I WAS BUSY,
NOW I'M NOT

Dedication

This book is dedicated to Holy Spirit, my best friend and the One who taught me the best way to leverage (multiply) my time is to give God more of it.

Key Messages

TIME is your LIFE.
When you waste your time, you waste your life.

To be spiritually healthy, you must ruthlessly eliminate hurry from your life.

Key Scripture

So teach us to number our days that we may gain a heart of wisdom. (Psalm 90:12)

An Elixir to Forever Change Your Mindset

There is an elixir in this book that if you dare to take a deep drink of it, will forever change your mindset and thought patterns about what you have believed time to be, while refreshing and strengthening you to the core of your inner being.

When you actually believe how precious a gift time is (that has equally been endowed to every man, woman, and child daily), only then can you begin to excel in leveraging time with all the nuggets packed in this book.

Proper understanding of these time principles coupled with the ability to hear God's voice and journal daily creates a laser focus for an extremely productive, healthy, and massively effective lifestyle bringing glory to God, and accomplishing far more than you ever thought possible, all with time to spare.

By focusing first and foremost daily on Abba and by getting His direction you can save great heartache and useless frenzied activity that looks good but accomplishes little.

Having the extra time also opens the door to be more relaxed and available, at the same time being more sensitive to Holy Spirit's direction.

This then releases the ability to recognize the dream portals when they open, and to aggressively pursue your destiny, all the while smashing the barriers holding you back from working with an intentional attitude of resting in faith in Him.

I believe countless people who are led of Holy Spirit, and who truly want to revolutionize their lives with ageless time redemption strategies, have an empowering toolkit placed in their hands!

I have watched Dr. Joseph Peck continue to excel with the abilities and talents the Lord has graciously imparted to him, and live life to the fullest with passion, always delivering as promised. His life exemplifies the time-tested truths in this excellent book, and it is a joy to know and work with him!

—Russel Stauffer
Master Joint Venture Broker

"In *I Was Busy, Now I'm Not*[TM], Dr. Joseph Peck, *The Time Doctor*[TM], provides eternal wisdom for one of life's greatest challenges —stewardship of our days. While God can redeem our days, why make it any harder for Him to do His job? Embrace the lessons in this book and you will be in partnership with God."

—Kevin W. McCarthy
America's Chief Leadership Officer
Author, *The On-Purpose Person: Making Your Life Make Sense*
www.on-purpose.com

"One of our biggest Dragons in life is procrastination. Dr. Joseph Peck will help you slay this Dragon in his new book, *I Was Busy, Now I'm Not*[TM]. You will learn how to be a master of your time and never let it enslave you again. This is a must read for every busy entrepreneur!"

—Lisa Jimenez M.Ed.
Author, *Dragon Slayer!* and *Conquer Fear!*
www.Rx-Success.com

"Dr. Joseph Peck is a dear friend of mine and we have worked together closely on several projects. I know he practices what is in *I Was Busy, Now I'm Not*[TM]. Many say 'time is money' and that is true to a point. According to Ecclesiastes 3:1-8, God never intended for time to be our master, but intended for us to master time. Dr. Peck has put together a masterpiece showing us how to master time in a simple practical way. As you read through this book, you will find principles and strategies that will bring acceleration and ease to your journey, you will find yourself in a place of rest, joy and satisfaction, and you will find yourself achieving more than you could ever imagine. This book is not only a must read but also a tool for life."

—John Burpee
Founder, John Burpee Ministries
www.johnburpee.com

"In *I Was Busy, Now I'm Not*[TM], Dr. Joseph Peck has issued a clarion call to value and appreciate our most precious commodity, time. The reader will discover helpful insights and practical coaching tools to master their time and leverage their life. Masterfully done! A must read for anyone desiring to redeem their days and make time matter."

—Janet G. Daughtry
Cofounder of Life Breakthrough Academy
and the Biblical Coaching Alliance
www.lifebreakthroughcoach.com
www.biblicalcoachingalliance.com

"Most people would see a massive and near-immediate impact in their lives if they understood and practiced some simple time management strategies. In *I Was Busy, Now I'm Not*™, Dr. Joseph Peck not only gives us the reason 'why' we need to change our thinking about time, but the 'how' we do it as well. And this guidance comes from a great student of these timeless principles. Joseph is truly a 'walks his talk' leader and teacher."

—**Vic Johnson**
Founder of AsAManThinketh.net
www.AsAManThinketh.net

"Dr. Joseph Peck sees possibilities everywhere. His desire and drive to help people through inspired insight is insatiable. You cannot work with Joseph without being encouraged to reach for more.

In *I Was Busy, Now I'm Not*™, Joseph inspires and equips you to seek God's counsel, walk in wisdom, make the most of your time and live with God's priorities in mind rather than reacting to life's demands. He helps you to recognize the strategic opportunities God places in your path, and avoid the trap of spoiling God's best by going after good things that keep you busy.

Value your time; it is a precious gift. Stay spiritually alert, and position yourself to recognize God incidences as wonderful opportunities that impact eternity and leave a valuable legacy. I encourage you to internalize the message of this book and discover how to be a good steward of your time and use it wisely."

—**Lynne Lee**
Breakthrough Life Coach and Coach Trainer
Author, *How To Hear God*
www.ChristianLifeCoaching.co.uk

"Dr. Joseph Peck is by far the greatest time management expert I have ever known. This new book is a masterpiece that will dramatically transform your life as you embrace and apply these treasured principles. The pages are filled with a lifetime of wisdom that can help you redeem time itself and live your life filled with quantum results."

—**Gary Beaton**
Executive Television and Film Producer
Founder, Transformation Glory Ministries
www.transformationglory.com

"Do you ever question: will my life matter? In his book *I Was Busy, Now I'm Not*™, Dr. Joseph Peck discusses concise targets to help you get on a life-changing track.

This book is easy to understand and gives helpful direction to shift your time to make your life matter starting today."

—**Wanda Ulrey**
Setting Captives Free

"Every now and again you come across a book with the potential to be a personal 'Game Changer,' a book that is a revelation to you, a book that appeared at exactly the right time, one that can change your life completely.....if you will let it.

Dr. Joseph's book *I Was Busy, Now I'm Not*™ is one of these. Packed with profound concepts, practical ideas, and useful tips and strategies, this book will change the way you think about time and its relationship to God's plans and purposes for your life. With his trademark passion, Joseph leaves no stone unturned in drawing our attention to our relationship with time.

Joseph also issues a challenge we all need to face. His proposition 'When you waste your time, you waste your life' can be deeply unsettling when you think about how you personally use time.

If *I Was Busy, Now I'm Not*™ has found its way into your hands then it is there for a reason. So thank God for His goodness, pay attention, and let it become a 'Game Changer' in some area of your life. It has done that for me."

—**Steve Connell**
Cofounder, Kingdom Business Builders
www.kingdombusinessbuilders.com

"I believe the most powerful statement in this book (besides the life changing experience that Dr. Joseph Peck experienced and he shared in this book) is the statement, 'If you waste your time, you waste your life.' This book is about helping people who want to know how to 'redeem their time.' It is practical, easy to read, and when applied to your life, there are life changing results that will help men and women achieve those goals that have not been realized. When you read this book and apply what he is telling you to do, you begin to believe that results are possible. Dr. Joseph Peck has experienced personally for himself the truths found in this book. I believe that God is going to use this book to help people of all ages to be able to reach their potential as they apply these truths. I am excited to see what God is going to do."

—**Chaplain Liz Danielsen**
Executive Director and President
Spiritual Care Support Ministries, Inc.
www.scsm.tv

"The first words that come to mind in reading this book are *uniquely you*. Joseph has taken the complex in life and made it simple. He uniquely clarifies how to identify where you are at in life and then causes you to see the next place to step. His writing is backed in humility of his own life's journey still in process. This book has caused an earthquake within me. It has permanently shifted my 'internal plates' to identify what is really important according to God and put me on a path to fulfill them. If you apply these clear principles, you will become *uniquely you* where Jesus shines forth."

—**Pastor Bobby Alger**
Senior Pastor, Crossroads Community Church
www.crossroadswinchester.com

"I have been blessed to hear Dr. Joseph Peck speak passionately on all the topics in *I Was Busy, Now I'm Not*™. But I consider this concisely written book a real treasure. You see, I love to study and underline. Studying (reading) any material for a period of time equal to the length of time required for verbally presenting the material results in significantly greater comprehension. You will read and reread this gem many times. Let's face it, we all backslide. But if you keep your copy of *I Was Busy, Now I'm Not*™ handy, you will re-sharpen your focus, spend more sacred time with God, hear His voice through daily journaling, define your destiny, and eliminate busyness. One copy will definitely not be enough!"

—**Virginia Morton**
Author, *Marching Through Culpeper*
www.marchingthroughculpeper.com

"From the CEO who needs direction, to the pastor who needs shepherding of their own, to the mom or dad who constantly seem to be looking for more hours in the day, *I Was Busy, Now I'm Not*™ has been carefully crafted to take even the most talented CEOs, business leaders, pastors, and work-at-home moms or dads to a higher level of purpose and effectiveness both personally and professionally. This book is written by a master coach who refuses to give pat answers. Dr. Peck exposes the multitude of potholes on the roads of life that slow you down and coaches you through the steps you need to take to personally discover what steps must be taken to reach your full potential."

—**Mark Jenkins**
Lead Pastor, Mountain View Community Church
www.mountainviewcc.net

"Deep within each of us is the secret and sometimes even hidden desire to be great – to be the 'more' our Creator has designed each of us to be. Yet too often, the inability to focus our time wisely can intercept our dreams causing us to live impotent lives—void of the impact we were designed to make. Dr. Joseph Peck provides an empowering and practical path to living out our dreams by focusing us with steely clarity on what is most important and freeing us to be who we were created to be."

—**Cheryl-Ann Needham**
Author, *Sound Alignment*
Cofounder, Global Stewards Initiative

"Joseph, I am thrilled to see you encouraging the art of two-way journaling. It took me forever to discover that God's voice generally comes as spontaneous thoughts. Likewise, it took me forever to learn to fix my eyes on Him during my quiet times, seeing Him at my right hand, as David did (Acts 2:25). I am glad to see you introducing people to these tools so they can more easily hear the voice of the Wonderful Counselor. Good job!"

—**Dr. Mark Virkler**
Author, *4 Keys to Hearing God's Voice*
Founder, Communion With God Ministries
President, Christian Leadership University
www.cwgministries.org
www.cluonline.com

"Are you over your head in the rat race? Do you wish you had more time? Are the years passing you by? Do you wonder what became of the dreams and goals you once had? If you answered 'Yes' to only one of these questions, I encourage you to read Dr. Joseph Peck's book, *I Was Busy, Now I'm Not*™. Dr. Peck will motivate you to slow down and reevaluate how you use your time. He will ignite the fire of your dreams and goals, and you will feel revitalized, challenged, and encouraged to move forward."

—**Yvonne Ortega**, LPC, LSATP, CCDVC
Bilingual Speaker, Author, Counselor, Teacher, Coach
www.yvonneortega.com
www.yvonneortega.net

"I have never met anyone like Dr. Joseph Peck. He is a phenomenal human being who lives out his soul purpose like no one else I know. No one who I personally know gets more done and is more passionate than Joseph Peck. While we were each created to live full, creative, passionate, purposeful lives, most of us instead have a bland, ordinary existence. This book gives the 'secrets' and real-life applications that can propel anyone from mere existence to a passionate and productive life! Thank you, Joseph for giving us the gift of *I Was Busy, Now I'm Not*™!"

—**Matt Gregory**
Senior Pastor, Soul Purpose Community Church
www.soulpurposechurch.org

"Joseph Peck has mastered time. He keeps in constant contact with Holy Spirit to guide his life and direct his unique gifts and talents to connect with and teach others. This book will launch you into a new energized zone, while giving you tools to eliminate hurry, prioritize, and step forward with the peace of Christ."

—**Judi G. Reid**
Author, *Rise Up! 71 Thoughts of Hope and Inspiration for Women of Value*
www.womenofvalue.org

"Dr. Peck has taken me to a whole new level in life. He is one of the best communicators that I know. Dr. Peck's enthusiasm for life and purpose is contagious and he is always helping to bring the best out of each of us. With his coaching and webinars, he clarifies our dreams and helps us create dream teams to fulfill our destinies."

—**Jack Stagman**
Founder and President, America Restored
www.americarestored.org

"I love reading books by other physicians. Luke may be the 'beloved physician,' but Dr. Peck is surely becoming the modern example of what anyone, including any physician, can become when they step into their God-given calling. I first began seriously thinking about how a person can have an impact when as a thirteen year old I was introduced to *How To Win Friends And Influence People* by Dale Carnegie. When, in my late 30's, I made a major change in my career, and moved away from clinical medicine into primarily ministry and business work, I was introduced to the Franklin Time Management system, now made world famous through the Franklin-Covey books and seminars. Now, approaching 65, but with bigger goals before me than ever, thanks in part to the impact of Dr. Peck and his coaching, I can only urge everyone to get hold of this book; read it and then read it again! This will not only change the way you think about time, it will change the way that you think about living!"

—**Tony Dale**, M.D.
Author and Entrepreneur
Founder of The Karis Group and The Health Co-Op
www.thekarisgroup.com
www.thehealthcoop.com

"It should come as no surprise to any Bible believing, Spirit-filled man or woman of God that we are truly living in the last days. So many of the signs have been seen in just the last few generations alone, with the re-formation of the nation of Israel, Jerusalem going back into the hands of the nation, and the rebelliousness and wickedness of humanity dramatically increasing. What we do with our time now will be an important investment into the final expansion of God's kingdom, and if we steward our time well and use it to the full extent that God wants us to use it, our part of His end-time story will be written well and we will receive those amazing words at the door of heaven 'well done my good and faithful servant.'

Not taking our time seriously is a recipe for a life of misery, disappointment, and failure. Books like this one should be read by anyone wanting to accomplish all that God has for them and truly live the life they were made to live and enjoy. Stay close to Dr. Peck as he is a great guide for that journey!"

—Chris Vercelli
Founder and Owner of Non-Fiction Fitness
www.nonfictionfitness.com

"Because Dr. Joseph Peck knows how important it is to get to our 'Why,' he has modeled the skill of saying 'No' to the good and 'Yes' to the best. Realigning our lives around that core question is the secret weapon that keeps us living on target with margins and room to breathe. This is no theory but a practical way out of your one step forward and two steps back. Your first right choice is not to be too busy to read it."

—Dr. Joseph Umidi
Founder, Lifeforming Leadership Coaching
www.lifeformingcoach.com

"For those of us who live busy, demanding lives, nothing is more important than being able to control our time, efforts, and outputs. That is the essence of this book, teaching us how to free up our time, simplify our lives, and to accomplish more than we ever thought possible.

When we leave the starting blocks of the day we should, as much as possible, have outlined and chartered our way, have clearly outlined our hoped for accomplishments, and have a view of the finish line in sight. This can be summed up in one prayerful word, 'FOCUS!'

Let us all begin by praying, 'Father, what is the one thing I can focus on today (this hour, this week, this month, this year) that will make everything else I do easier or unnecessary? Teach me to focus and be on-purpose, and to understand that being on-purpose begins with a decision to be identified with Christ because if I win the rat race, I am still a rat.'

This book will help us do all those things and it will unlock for us little truisms such as: when you stay connected with God, fruit happens; the simplest solution is often the best; the one thing that keeps people from successfully living the life they dream of is fear."

—**Maj. Gen. Jerry R. Curry**
U.S. Army, Ret.
Author, *The Dream Continues*

"To everything there is a season and a time to every purpose under the heaven. (Ecclesiastes 3:1) In his book *I Was Busy, Now I'm Not*™, Dr. Joseph Peck tackles the subject of one of the greatest resources that we will ever be given in life— TIME. Like the great and wise King Solomon, Dr. Peck gives us practical insights and wisdom on stewarding time in new and effective ways. Since most people are seeking to be more productive in life, they have studied the many ways to increase financially, spiritually, socially and physically, but no one has conquered the challenge of how to add more than 24 hours to a day! Since we cannot add time to our day, we must learn to manage time and leverage it in new and productive ways, avoiding stress, burnout and depression in the process. This is not just another book about 'time management.' This is a book about God's strategies for being productive with time and how not to lose our relationship with God in the process. Only a person who really knows God, like Dr. Joseph Peck, could creatively map out a book like this. What a great work, and what a great gift to us all! Thank you Dr. Peck."

—**Dr. Gordon E. Bradshaw**
President, Global Effect Movers and Shakers Network (GEMS)
www.gemsnetwork.org
Author, *Authority for Assignment:
Releasing the Mantle of God's Government in the Marketplace*

"Dr. Joseph Peck is my Breakthrough Life Coach. Under his guidance, I discerned my Kingdom Assignment to connect every Kingdom Enterprise in the world with a General Counsel who will be as Joseph was to Pharaoh, namely, God's wisdom channel into the enterprise. *I Was Busy, Now I'm Not*™ contains tools I can use in fulfilling that Assignment! Thank you, Dr. J!"

—**Michael Oswald**
Managing Partner, innovaCounsel, LLP
www.innovacounsel.com

"Dr. Joseph Peck has helped me regain my focus and balance as a Christian businessman. I have not found such wisdom in modern times to match the 'common sense' that Dr. Peck brings to addressing our over-worked and over-stressed corporate lives. I have personally found Joseph to be a caring, loving, gentle version of what a true Christian life coach should be. I am more focused on Christ and His will for my life after applying Dr. Peck's 'balanced' approach to business and life. Psalm 23:1-3"

—**Scott Shofner**
CEO, Secure Leverage Group Inc.
Private Equity/Hedge Fund Manager

"We live in a hurry-sick culture with little time to rest, reflect, and do our own research. The Founding Fathers of America understood the importance of having ample time to reflect and build strong relationships. In addition to helping you slow down and be a better steward with your time, this book will draw you nearer to God."

—**Stephen McDowell**
President, Providence Foundation
Biblical Worldview University
www.providencefoundation.com

"While reading through Dr. Joseph Peck's new book *I was Busy, Now I'm Not*^{TM}, I can't help but feel that it would not be an understatement to say that this is one of the most important texts you will ever read in life, aside from the Bible!

Learning to not only value but manage time is something that most entrepreneurs are willing to spend huge fortunes on, yet I can personally say that there's no seminar I ever attended, or document I ever read, that taught me more on the art of treasuring and skillfully investing in what is to be considered the most sacred and valuable resource in life—time!

I had the blessing of personally connecting with Dr. Joseph Peck at a time of an important transition in my life, as I was coming out of a severe burn out and two heart attacks that forced me to slow down the fast pace of years of full time missionary activities. He came alongside me as an expert life coach and helped me reset my lifestyle in a balanced form so that I could move forward with a healthy sense of priorities and values in life. Thank you Joseph, I would not be where I am today, if it hadn't been for your patient and skillful expertise."

—**Renato Amato**
Founder, Healing Broken Hearts
Life Breakthrough Coach & Biblical Coach Trainer
www.renatoamato.com

"Joseph and I have been friends and colleagues for many years. It was one of those amazing, once-in-a-lifetime relationships where each of us contributed massively to the other's growth and development surrounding skill sets ranging from life coaching to Internet marketing and even to personal and spiritual accountability. In my book, he is the poster child for 'passion.' I have nothing but the greatest admiration and respect for the integrity and values of Dr. Joseph. His new book *I Was Busy, Now I'm Not*™ is simply the logical next step in his desire to better the lives of those who come in contact with him."

—Dr. Jerry Graham
Cofounder, The Coaching Pair
www.thecoachingpair.com

"Thank you Dr. Joseph! I have been so inspired reading your book *I Was Busy, Now I'm Not*™. You are an absolutely amazing man of God! You also have a huge capacity to put others first with a humble servant's heart. Thank you for being such an amazing example of living what you teach. In your book you point out that time is the most valuable asset we have and the vital importance of stewarding our time wisely. It is an honor to know you as a brother in Christ and as a friend! Thank you for the amazing impact you are having on my life, the Body of Christ, as well as others in the marketplace! *Dr. Time*, I might add that any time spent with you or reading your book is quality time!"

—Charlie Fisher
CEO of Guiding Business Transitions
www.gbtiam.com

"As the founder of the Christian Financial Concepts ministry, I am passionate about educating Christians to make wise and successful decisions in matters related to giving, financial management, investments, and asset stewardship. In his book *I Was Busy, Now I'm Not*™, Dr. Joseph Peck addresses the issue of stewarding time, your most valuable asset. He is a master at teaching how to redeem your time to live a focused, productive, and purposeful life. Reading this book was a game changer for me. I hope it will be the same for you and those you love. This would be a wonderful gift for your pastor, your co-workers, and your family. They will love you for it!"

—Dr. Tom Barrett
President, Golden Art Treasures, LLC
www.GoldenArtTreasures.com
Founder, Christian Financial Concepts
www.ChristianFinancialConcepts.com

"Dr. Joseph Peck is known as *The Time Doctor*™ and after reading *I Was Busy, Now I'm Not*™, it is clear he has a prescription for every person no matter where they are in life. If applied as directed, this book will change your life.

The truths in this book will unlock the sometimes dormant reality that your life has an eternal impact for you and others. It empowered me to make changes, some small, some great, so I could live each day with intentional purpose.

This book will be integral for you to live a fulfilling, passionate, and contagious life. Each day matters and when viewed from an eternal perspective, you are equipped to make each day powerful and effective. This book is a key for everyone looking for clarity, direction, and purpose for their lives or to expand their capacity. Joseph shows you it is never too late to make a fresh start and change direction. What greater joy than to know and live out your purpose from this day forward."

—**Michelle Bravenboer**
Founder, Mad Cow Ministries
Author, *Together We Walk Alone*
www.michellebravenboer.com

"I recommend *I Was Busy, Now I'm Not*^{TM} to Christians who feel too busy, always behind, and rushed. Dr. Peck does a good job of identifying the problems of busyness and the benefits of not being busy. More specifically he does a good job of imparting that God has a plan for each of us and to be able to hear and understand His plan. In order to do this we must live moment by moment in an intimate relationship with Him, seeking His will for our lives and building margin into our lives to be able to carry out His mission for us on this earth (i.e., our destiny revealed). Many aspire to know and understand God's will, but few actually take the time to make the time. Dr. Peck's book will be invaluable to those seeking a deeper walk with Christ and learning to let Him reign in all of our being, beginning with the surrender of 'time' to His Lordship. Dr. Peck's book will give insight and strategy on how to get started on the journey to less busyness and more intimate time with Father God. Thank you Dr. Peck for being an example and willing to share your journey. Blessings for a continued deeper and closer walk with Him!"

—**Don Morley**
Successful entrepreneur empowering other entrepreneurs

"This invaluable book takes readers by the hand, with simple step-by-step instructions and common-sense help they can use and benefit from if they discipline themselves and apply the principles taught. Dr. Peck has a down-to-earth, generous spirit and shares his own story with candor and humility, thus letting you know you are not alone in your time challenges. Those who take the instructions seriously and follow them will see a change of habits and positive outcomes that impact not just the here-and-now but eternity also."

—**Rich and Barbara Freeman**
Front Royal, VA

"We believe Dr. Joseph is a CULTURE CHANGER with an innate ability to coach and help incubate your dream and surround you with an extraordinary team to capture its essence and see you unleashed to accomplish that for which you are created for."

—**Russel Stauffer**, Master Joint Venture Strategist
Glenisaah Stauffer, President of the Embassy Group

"In his life transforming book, *I Was Busy, Now I'm Not*^{TM}, Dr. Joseph Peck, one of God's chosen generals for this generation, shares why we need to change our thinking about time, and provides invaluable time management strategies that the reader can apply into their life to reap a positive outcome to maximize their life without limits!"

—**Mercy Abbey**
Coach, Speaker, Author, Entrepreneur
Rhema Preserve Global
www.coachmercy.com

"Joseph is the Maestro making the entire orchestra speak with one voice. God has called him and given him the gifts and talent to take so many different individuals (instruments and sounds) and blend them together, so disciplined and so coordinated into 'sound alignment.' Working with Joseph is truly an incredible experience as he has the God-given gifts to help raise people up to be who God created them to be. Joseph really is *Dr. Breakthrough*. He has a creative gift that few others have."

—**Larry Tyler**
Founder and CEO, Up Your Business
www.upyourbusiness.biz

"Dr. Joseph Peck is a thought leader for his generation. Each person needs someone who comes alongside them and believes in them and their dreams. Dr. Peck is such a person. This simple act of belief starts a process of actions. Dr. Peck has a gift of formulating dreams into goals and steps that day-by-day become God-given destiny. He has an excellent way of establishing purpose and eliminating time wasters from the daily schedule. His teaching helped me realize what a gift my time is. As a result, I now take the necessary steps to achieve God's best for my life. If you feel overwhelmed and want more time for what matters most, this book is a must read."

—**Linda Zobel**
Author, *Accepted and Free*

"In the 31st Psalm, David states: 'my times are in Your hands.' In this gem of a book you will learn how to get control of your life, free yourself from over commitment, have ample time for yourself and your family, overcome procrastination, unlock the door of your personal destiny, and discover God's plan for your life. Your first step is reading this important book by Dr. Peck."

—**Richard W. Groux, Jr.**
Chairman, Christian Stewardship Ministries
www.csmin.org

"Dr. Joseph Peck, aka *The Time Doctor^{TM}*, delivers an over-the counter, easy-to-swallow, fast-acting prescription for the masses in his latest blockbuster book, *I Was Busy, Now I'm Not^{TM}*. This simple, powerful truth and its implications for every person, stirs something deep within our spirits and echoes a universal heart cry of humanity. Dr. Peck, a highly-trained, well-paid, successful and hard-working medical professional, unpacks and downloads a lifetime of wisdom and freedom from his own journey and transition from the brink of burnout to the peak of passion and performance. As a leading contrarian voice in the lineage of Henry David Thoreau and Warren Buffet, offering an alternative and antidote to the modern day rat race syndrome of human existence, and lives of quiet desperation, Dr. Peck probes deeply about what matters most and how we can take back control of our time and our lives. This modest- and unpretentious-sounding title is anything but that as every chapter is loaded with nuggets of revelation, inspiration, hope and personal testimony. Buy the first copy for yourself, and other copies for those you love."

—**Dr. Bruce Cook**
Chairman, Kingdom Congressional International Alliance
Author, *Aligning with the Apostolic*
www.kcialliance.org

I WAS BUSY, NOW I'M NOT

CHANGING THE WAY YOU THINK ABOUT
TIME

JOSEPH PECK, M.D.
THE TIME DOCTOR™

NEW YORK

I WAS BUSY, NOW I'M NOT
Changing the Way You Think About Time

Published in New York, New York, by Morgan James Publishing. Morgan James and The Entrepreneurial Publisher are trademarks of Morgan James, LLC.
www.MorganJamesPublishing.com

The Morgan James Speakers Group can bring authors to your live event. For more information or to book an event visit The Morgan James Speakers Group at www.TheMorganJamesSpeakersGroup.com.

Notice and Disclaimer: This publication, its author, and publisher expressly disclaim any expressed or implied warranties.

In this book, I give you the best advice I can to help you see the value of your time and to be a good steward with that. While I have seen these tips and strategies work for many people I have coached, I cannot guarantee they will work for you. That will depend on your ability to understand what I am saying and to follow my instructions as I intend.

Quotations of the Bible in this book are from the public domain.

Unless indicated otherwise, all scriptures are from the New King James Version (NKJV) of the Bible © 1982 by Thomas Nelson, Inc. All rights reserved. Used by permission.

A **free** eBook edition is available
with the purchase of this print book.

CLEARLY PRINT YOUR NAME ABOVE IN UPPER CASE

Instructions to claim your free eBook edition:
1. Download the BitLit app for Android or iOS
2. Write your name in **UPPER CASE** on the line
3. Use the BitLit app to submit a photo
4. Download your eBook to any device

ISBN 978-1-63047-294-8 paperback
ISBN 978-1-63047-295-5 eBook
ISBN 978-1-63047-296-2 hardcover
Library of Congress Control Number:
2014941657

Cover Design by:
Rachel Lopez
www.r2cdesign.com

In an effort to support local communities, raise awareness and funds, Morgan James Publishing donates a percentage of all book sales for the life of each book to Habitat for Humanity Peninsula and Greater Williamsburg.

Get involved today, visit
www.MorganJamesBuilds.com

Habitat
for Humanity®
Peninsula and
Greater Williamsburg
Building Partner

CONTENTS

FOREWORD

Rarely does a life changing revelation from God happen to you. When it does, you are simultaneously grateful and excited. Grateful because you know your life has been changed by God forever and excited to see what God then has in store for you. The Bible tells us that God can send leaders after His own heart into our lives. When they are sent to you by God, they lead you with knowledge and understanding.

"Then I will give you shepherds after my own heart, who will lead you with knowledge and understanding." (Jeremiah 3:15, NIV)

There are many gifted people in this world and I am thankful to God for all of them. It is wonderful when someone who is gifted and talented is recommended to you. That person can be of great help to you. However, it is extremely valuable and extraordinarily rare for God to send a gifted and talented person Himself into your life.

This is what God is revealing to us through Jeremiah 3:15. This person can only be given to you by God, who says *"I will give you shepherds after my own heart, who will lead you with knowledge and understanding."*

In the entire Bible, there is only one man, with the exception of Jesus Christ, that God describes as *"a man after mine own heart, which shall fulfill all my will."* (Acts 13:22, KJV). That man was "David, the son of Jesse."

There will never be another David that God says *"shall fulfil all my will,"* but God does say *"I will give you shepherds after my own heart who will lead you with knowledge and understanding."* This too is very valuable and very rare.

Dr. Joseph Peck, M.D. is such a man, a rare gift from God and his book glorifies God and will bless your life tremendously.

God can do anything and I pray He uses Dr. Peck's book to not only change how you view time, but in so doing, change the world, one person at a time, perhaps beginning with you.

—**Rick Saunders**
Cofounder, Lord and Saunders Real Estate
An ordinary life Jesus Christ changed forever
www.lordandsaunders.com

PREFACE

"Keep the fire lit. Each of us has a fire in our hearts for something. Find it and keep it lit."
—Mary Lou Retton

Let us dream together for a few minutes!

Imagine you are walking along the road of life and stumble across a dream coach who completely changes the course of your life by believing in you and the big dreams within you.

Imagine that dream coach shares a few simple secrets to free up one hour of your time each day. You in turn invest that extra seven hours of time each week doing things you enjoy the most and that make the biggest difference.

Imagine that dream coach helps you craft your perfect day and lay out a plan to move toward that each week.

Imagine how good you feel as you simplify your complicated life and have time for what matters most.

Imagine the new friendships you are building, the new places you are going, and the new things you are able to do.

Life without limits—that is what this is about. You being fully you, unleashed to accomplish the great things you were created for.

And yes, this is really possible if you have the right coach and mentor to help guide you along the way. A coach is a person walking with you to help you achieve your goals and dreams! If you allow me, I can be that dream coach for you.

I am passionate about creating a movement empowering dreams of millions of people around the world. And you can be one of those. Your first step is to read or listen to this book and meditate on it. And your second step is to stay connected with me by subscribing to my blog at www.iwasbusynowimnot.com.

The purpose of this book is to plant seeds of ideas in your mind and heart to dramatically change the way you think about time. As you redeem your precious gift of time and become more focused, you will be enabled to accomplish far more than you ever thought possible.

Today Your Life Will Change Forever!

Your mind is being expanded to the dimensions of new thought and it will never retract to its original size or shape!

Do you know time is your life? When you waste your time, you waste your life.

Let me ask you:

- Does your time seem to be in short supply?
- Have you had enough of feeling overwhelmed?
- Are you ready to find time for what matters most?

If so, this book will help you discover how to:

- Simplify your complicated life
- Make time for what matters most
- Live your big dreams

To live your big dreams as God intended, you must get a handle on your time. As *The Time Doctor*^{TM}, I can help you be a good steward with your time.

I am passionate about this subject of redeeming the time because for the first 20 years of my career, my time and life were not my own and I was not living my dream.

Yes, I earned a good living and had lots of creature comforts, but I was trapped in a box in a box in a box (i.e., in the operating room in a hospital in my community). When I finally broke out of that, I felt like I had been let out of jail after 20 years. For the first time in my adult life, I finally got a taste of true time freedom and I was determined never to give that up.

Before we get started talking about the value of time, know that I have been praying for you.

Pray this prayer out loud as a declaration for the next seven days, expecting God to answer this prayer for you. I think you might be amazed at what happens.

Heavenly Father, thank You for preparing and guiding Dr. Peck to share this important message with me to release Your wisdom, knowledge, and understanding regarding time. Please open my eyes of understanding to receive everything You want me to know and have. I acknowledge that I need Your help to change my thinking to change my life. I surrender all that I am, all that I have, and all that I do to You. Remove what does not belong in my life and bless all that remains. Grant me the courage to face the impossible, love that overcomes fear, and the tangible presence of God that makes the supernatural a daily experience! In Jesus' name, I pray. Amen.

As you read this book, be aware that when I include two-way prayers (i.e., dialogues with the Lord), things I sense the Lord saying to me are in *italics*. I often refer to these as **WFJ—Words From Jesus**. While I do not profess to be 100% accurate, I would rather be right 80% of the time and take action with a heart to obey God than to always question if I am really hearing from God and not do what I sense He is prompting me to do. This comes down to trust. Jesus says, *"**My sheep hear My voice**, and I know them, and they follow Me." (John 10:27)*

CHAPTER 1

THE VALUE OF TIME

Looking Beyond for Perspective

When you change your thinking, you change your life.

Most people do not value their time. They think they do, but if you carefully observe their behavior, you will notice priorities out of order, lack of focus, and numerous ways they waste their time.

In May 2011, I launched my very first *I Was Busy, Now I'm Not*™ coaching program. Two of the people who signed up to participate were Steve and Tara Connell from New Zealand. I had never met them before, but during this four-week virtual training we became good friends. I learned Steve and Tara are the cofounders of Kingdom Business Builders.

Within a week or two of starting this group coaching program, it became very obvious to me that Steve and Tara were master communicators and extraordinary coaches in their own right.

So even though they had paid to be part of my coaching program, I asked them to facilitate the discussion for two of the weekly webinars. During one of those webinars, Tara shared an anonymous poem titled "The Value of Time." That really resonated with my spirit. Here it is:

Imagine there is a bank that:

- Credits your account each morning with $86,400
- Carries over no balance from day to day

- Allows you to keep no cash balance
- Every evening cancels whatever part of the amount you had failed to use during the day

What would you do? Draw out every cent of course!

Well, every one of us has such a bank. Its name is TIME.

Every morning it credits you with 86,400 seconds.

Every night it writes off as lost whatever of this you have failed to invest to good purpose.

It carries over no balance.
It allows no overdraft.
Each day it opens a new account for you.
Each night it burns the records of the day.

If you fail to use the day's deposits, the loss is yours. There is no going back. There is no drawing against "tomorrow." You must live in the present on today's deposits.

Invest it so as to get from it the utmost in health, happiness, and success. The clock is running. Make the most of today.

The takeaway message for this poem is: "**Today is the precious present.**" Tomorrow never comes. It is always today. To make the most of your life, you must make the most of your time today.

A Divine Encounter that Radically Changed My Life

On January 21, 2010, I had the privilege of hosting a webinar with Rick Grubbs titled "Redeeming the Time." That was by far the best presentation about time I have ever heard.

Rick is the founder of *Life Changing Seminars* and *Redeeming the Time* radio. He may well be the foremost expert in the world teaching about redeeming the time, having shared his presentation more than 1,500 times in at least 49 states and 20 countries.

It was Rick Grubbs who opened my eyes of understanding to see "time is your life." It was Rick who taught me, "When you waste your time, you waste your life." And I have never been the same since.

At the beginning of his presentation, Rick explained what it means to redeem the time. "Redeem" means "to rescue from going to waste" and "time" is "the passing of life."

If you ask a group of people, "Does anybody here plan on wasting your life?" nobody says "yes." However, if you ask, "How many of you will likely waste a little time this coming week?", every single person listening is guilty to some degree.

This reveals a tactic of the devil. He tries to make you think that somehow there is a difference between time on one hand, and life itself on the other. If he can do that, the result is you will not properly value your time. If you do not see your time as life, it is easy to waste a minute of it.

Now, if that happens 60 times through your day, you have wasted an hour. 24 hours slip by and a day has gone unredeemed. This can easily turn into a week, a month, or maybe even a year without you doing anything significant for God. You may simply drift in and out of the different seasons of your life without ever really embracing what God has for you.

Then one day you wake up an old man or an old woman, looking back on life frustrated and thinking, "Where did it go? What happened to all those things I wanted to do for God as a young person?" This happens when you fail to realize that when you waste your time, you really are wasting your life. A wasted life is simply an accumulation of a lot of wasted time.

The starting point to redeeming your time is to realize time is your life and it is impossible to waste your time without also wasting your life. Since nobody wants to wake up from the tragedy of a wasted life behind them, let us look next at the question of why it is so important to redeem the time. Unless you have a firm understanding of the why, you will not follow through with the how.

Six reasons why it is so important to redeem your time

1. Time is limited
2. Death is certain

3. Our use of time brings eternal consequences
4. Time is not recoverable
5. Time is our most valuable earthly possession
6. We must give an account of how we spend our time

Let us take a closer look at each of these.

1. Time is limited.

Time is a limited resource. Whenever you have a limited resource, you must be careful how you use it. Let me illustrate what I mean.

Have you ever had a time in your life when you were short on money? Think back to the last time things were tight financially and you got hungry. Did you rush down to the most expensive restaurant in town and plop down a $100 bill saying, "Keep the change?" No, no, no, no, no.

During those lean times, you stay home and eat. You may even get some beans and rice because you realize that money is in short supply and you have to be careful how you spend it.

God wants you to have kind of attitude toward your time because it is short supply. On average, a person in America lives about 80 years. If you get nothing else from this book, have a clear picture in your mind of how short 80 years really is.

To do that, draw a simple chart with time at the bottom. Think of this chart as a picture of your life. At the left, write zero and on the right, write 80. Now place a little mark on the chart wherever you find yourself.

As you do that, consider very carefully how much time has already gone by. If you are 40 years old, half of your life is gone and you are entering the third quarter of your life. If you are 60 old, three-quarters of your life is gone and you are entering the last quarter of your life.

But there is another reason why this chart demands your attention and that is the "snowball effect." If you went to the top of a snow-covered hill, made a little snowball, and gave it a push, the snowball would get bigger and bigger as it rolled down the hill. And it would also go faster and faster, gaining momentum. That is the way your life is. As you get older, life seems to go by faster and faster.

So the point is this—**whatever God has put you in this world to do, you better get started doing it**. Do not waste another minute.

2. Death is certain.

There will come a time in your life when you have no more time. The problem is that most people think and live their lives as if death is far off and if it does happen soon, it will happen to someone else.

Let me illustrate this with a story. A young man is at home and one day hears a knock at the door. When he answers the door, it is Death. Surprised, the young man says, "Wait a minute, Death. I am a young man now. Can you get the old man down the street? He has had a full life and I have not." Death says, "Okay, I think I will do that. The next time I come back for you, I will give you a warning so you can get ready."

Well, the young man is relieved. He cherishes his time and life for a while like one does after a close encounter with Death. But as time goes on, he forgets about Death. He goes through his twenties and gets a good education. In his thirties, he raises a nice family. In his forties and fifties, he climbs the ladder of success doing quite well.

Then one day when he is an old man, he hears another knock on the door. "Wait a minute, Death. You did not keep your promise. You told me you would give me a warning so I could get ready."

Death replies, "Just a moment, old man. Remember that time when you were in your twenties and you had to get your first pair of glasses? Or remember the time you were in your thirties and tried to play basketball with the teenagers and could not keep up like you used to? Look at your face. Look at your hair. Those are not the features of a young man. They are the features of an old man. I did not give you just one warning. I gave you warnings every day. You just would not listen and now it is time for you to come with me."

The goal here is to emphasize the brevity of life. As a result of that, the desire to redeem the time is stronger.

3. Our use of time brings eternal consequences.

The most important reason to redeem your time is because **the way you use your time today is going to have consequences for all of eternity**. Galatians 6:7 states, *"Do not be deceived, God is not mocked; for whatever a man sows, that he will also reap."* This scripture is saying that life operates on the Law of the Harvest—that what you plant today, you will harvest. In other words, what you do with your time today is going to bring consequences in your future.

Now this sowing-reaping, cause-effect relationship seems easy to understand for most of us until we apply it to eternity. We tend to think through this process of sowing and reaping with regard to our time only to the point of death. But death is not where the consequence of how you spend your time today is going to end. That is where the real consequences will all begin.

During your life on earth, you are sowing, but then for all of eternity, you will be reaping the consequences of what you chose to plant in this very short season of time. We all have a hard time understanding this matter of eternity.

Unless you make that connection between how you spend your time today and the eternal consequences, you will not ever have the frame of reference you really need to redeem the time.

As Rick Grubbs struggled with this issue years ago, he asked God if there was some way he could give people a picture of eternity so they could see and get a handle on it.

Holy Spirit led Rick to the Guinness Book of World Records to try to find the largest number that anyone has ever officially named. One of the numbers he found was "ten duotrigintillion." That is a "1" followed by one hundred "0s" or 10 to the 100th power.

10,000,000,000,000,000,000,000,000,000,000,000,000,000,000,000,
000,000,000,000,000,000,000,000,000,000,000,000,000,000,000,00
0,000,000

To understand how big this number is, think about the national debt of the United States of America, which is trillions of dollars or "1" followed by twelve "0s."

One trillion = 1,000,000,000,000

Several years ago when Rick was in the state of New York, a math professor came up to him after his presentation and told Rick his team tried to calculate the number of atoms in the entire known universe. Their estimate was a "1" followed by 85 zeros.

For a born-again follower of Jesus, the concept of eternity is very encouraging. However, there is another side to this big number because the Bible is clear that everybody will not go to heaven. This is the most tragic thought for people who die without Jesus Christ in their hearts.

The reality of this was made very clear to Rick a few years ago when someone told him this true story. That man was driving down a road in the state of Georgia when a semi-truck in front of him lost control and crashed into a ditch. When the man ran down into the ditch, he found the driver of the truck trapped inside the cab.

The man tried to help the truck driver get out and so did some other men who arrived at the scene of the accident. In a few minutes the cab burst into flames and began to burn very intensely where the driver was. The men at the scene tried everything to get that man out, even to the point of burning their own skin and clothing. But they soon realized that the twisted metal from that wreck held him in a way that made it impossible to get him out. There was simply nothing else they could do but step back and watch in horror as that man burned alive in front of them.

As the truck driver burned alive, he screamed out in agony, "Someone please, please shoot me. Don't make me die like this." Obviously no one did that. A few more moments passed and the driver begged one more time before dying, "Someone please throw a rock at my head. Knock me out. Do not let me die this way."

The man who told Rick this story said he and the other men who witnessed that vomited because of the horror of what they had seen. That was a tragic way to die, yet that man's suffering probably only lasted about 10 minutes before he lost consciousness and died.

But can you imagine someone suffering like that for 10 years in hell? That is already beyond my comprehension. What about suffering like that for 10,000 years or 10,000,000 (ten million) years? Most Christians do not have a sense of urgency about their lives or saving people from hell.

A British skeptic once said to a Christian, "You Christians do not really believe the Bible is true. If I really believed for one moment that there was a place as horrible as what Jesus described, I would get on my hands and knees and crawl on broken glass all the way across my country to warn one person of a place like hell. But you do not do that. So, you do not really believe it either."

Before I move on to the fourth reason it is so important to redeem your time, let me ask you, "If you were to die this very second, do you know for sure, beyond a shadow of a doubt, that you would go to Heaven?"

If "yes," that is great. If not, know that God loves you and has a wonderful plan for your life. Let me share what the holy Bible says about salvation and eternal life.

The book of Romans states, *"for all have sinned and fall short of the glory of God,"* It also says *"For the wages of sin is death, but the gift of God is eternal life in Christ Jesus our Lord."* And *"For whoever calls on the name of the LORD shall be saved."* You are a "whoever."

If you want to receive the free gift of eternal life that comes only through Jesus Christ, then say this prayer out loud if you mean it with all your heart:

"Lord Jesus, I invite you into my heart this day. Forgive me of my sin, wash me, and cleanse me of all unrighteousness. Set me free. Jesus, thank You for dying for me. I believe that You are raised from the dead and are coming back again for me. Fill me with Holy Spirit. Give me a passion for the lost, a hunger for the things of God, and a holy boldness to preach the gospel of Jesus Christ. I am saved. I am born again. I am forgiven and I am on my way to Heaven because I have Jesus in my heart."

4. Time is not recoverable.

You can never recover your time once it is gone. That is the nature of time. You use it or lose it.

For what is your life? It is even a vapor that appears for a little time and then vanishes away. (James 4:14)

If we live long enough, there comes a point in most of our lives when we no longer think about our life in terms of how far we have come, but rather in terms of how far we have left to go. Eventually, your reference point changes. You no longer look back and think how many birthdays you have had, but rather start looking in the other direction and think about how many more birthdays you will have.

Most people do not see time as something they accumulate. Typically, they see time as something they are using or something they have left. In Psalm 90, King David prayed to God, *"So teach us to number our days that we may gain a heart of wisdom."* The sooner you start counting your days, the wiser you will be with how you steward your time.

Psalm 90:12 is a key verse for Matt Gregory, my former pastor and coaching group partner. Matt actually has a five gallon clear container full of marbles, each one representing a day of his life. Each day he removes one of the marbles from the container to remind him of how quickly life is passing. This also reminds him that he can never get his marbles (days) back after they are gone.

5. Time is our most valuable earthly possession.

One of the best examples of this in history is Queen Elizabeth I of England. She was the wealthiest person in the world in her day, like the Bill Gates of her era. She had everything money could buy. And yet, when it came time for Queen Elizabeth to die, she said, "I would give all of my kingdom for one more moment of time." Queen Elizabeth finally understood the value of time, but it was too late.

6. We must give an account of how we spend our time.

In Matthew 12:36, Jesus says, *"But I say to you that for every idle word men may speak, they will give account of it in the day of judgment."*

I would like to emphasize two points here. The first is that there will be a day of judgment for each of us. And second, you and I are going to have to give an account to God of how we used our time.

This scripture is not saying there is no place in life for any kind of rest, recreation, or relaxation. But what Jesus is emphasizing is the importance of being intentional with every moment that God gives you.

Four Practical Ways to Redeem Your Time

1. Learn how to wake up and get up.

Getting up early is not easy for most people. However, your devotional life and your walk with God are going to rise or fall based on your ability to consistently get up on time and spend that morning time with God. It is important to win the battle of "mind over mattress."

Would you like an extra two-week vacation next year? Sure you would. Well, if you get up just 15 minutes earlier each day, consistently every day for one year, you will add more than 92 hours of waking time to your life, which is more than two 40-hour work weeks.

Some people say they are not a morning person. I think that is an excuse. There are two common reasons people do not feel like getting up early in the morning. The first is they go to bed too late. And the second is that they are not living a focused, purposeful life that leads to passion.

2. Get organized.

There are two things to organize—your time and your space. Your space is where you live and work. Removing clutter from your physical environment helps you think more clearly and brings more peace.

Getting organized is crucial to the matter of redeeming the time. Rick Grubbs defines "organization" as arranging your life so God can use you to your fullest potential. He recommends investing in some type of simple organizer, be it electronic or paper.

I personally plan out each week before it begins using a simple document with each day of the week listed and the major things I am to do each day. You can keep that weekly planner in a notebook or on your computer with software such as Microsoft Word. When you write things down, you are more likely to follow through.

3. Identify and eliminate time wasters.

The devil has three goals for your life—to steal, kill and destroy (John 10:10). In other words, the devil is a thief. Now, thieves will always go after the most valuable thing they can get their hands on. We have already established that time is your most valuable resource. So the devil can keep ruining your life and rob your joy simply by keeping you too busy to do what God is asking you to do.

All day long, the devil and his companions are sending people and circumstances in your life to distract you and steal away your time. But if you can spot a thief before he gets to your valuables, you can do whatever is necessary to protect those valuables.

How do you spot a thief of time? The answer is by asking two simple questions before committing your time to any activity. This first question is, "**What is going to be the fruit or the result of this activity in five years?**" That simply means, five years from today, is this thing going to make any difference if I do it or if I don't? If the answer is "no," then leave it alone and do something else that will make a difference.

The second question to ask is, "**What will be the fruit of this activity in eternity?**" This question is similar to the first, but probes much deeper.

It is only what you do for Jesus Christ that is going to last forever when you invest your time. When you invest your time for eternal treasure, you never lose because they last forever.

When you get right down to it, there are only three ways you can invest time that matter in eternity—God, His Word and people. The challenge I want to leave everybody with is simply this: Let us learn how to focus our time on those three things—God, His Word and people. Leave off everything else that does not directly contribute to one of those three. If you do that, you are going to redeem the time.

4. Conquer procrastination.

Rick Grubbs says the number one time-waster is procrastination. He says **procrastination is putting off until later what God wants me to do right now**.

Rick actually has four different parts to his seminar series about redeeming the time. The first is the introduction. The second deals with why we procrastinate and how we can overcome that through God's Word and God's principles.

The number one thing that keeps lost people lost is being convinced that they have more time. A second reason for this is that most Christians are convinced there will be another opportunity to share the gospel message a little further down the road. They might say, "When I have more time, or when I have more money, or when my kids are grown, or when I retire, or when this happens, I will start serving God full-time and get involved with my local church." But the truth is, tomorrow never comes. It is always today.

The key to overcoming procrastination is to ask this focusing question each moment of each day, **"Father, what do you want me to do right now?"** Then do whatever you hear. When you are finished with that task, inquire of the Lord again. Learn to stay in constant conversation with God. Make a commitment to developing that habit.

To learn more about Rick Grubbs and his outstanding teachings, please visit www.lifechangingseminars.com.

Prayer Power

Abba, Father, thank You for the precious gift of time. Help me to understand the value of time and to redeem the time you have allotted to me. Teach me to number my days that I may gain a heart of wisdom (Psalm 90:12). Teach me what it means to seek Your kingdom and Your righteousness first each day (Matthew 6:33). And lead me in the way everlasting (Psalm 139:24). Amen and hallelujah!

Study Guide

Questions:

Q: What does it mean to "redeem the time"?
A: At the beginning of his presentation, Rick Grubbs explained what it means to redeem the time. "Redeem" means "to rescue from going to waste" and "time" is "the passing of life."

Q: How is "procrastination" defined in this chapter?

A: Rick Grubbs says the number one time-waster is procrastination. He defines procrastination as putting off until later what God wants me to do right now.

Simple Action Step:

Make the commitment, right now, that you will overcome procrastination by asking this focusing question each moment of each day, "Father, what do you want me to do right now?" Then do whatever you hear. When you are finished with that task, inquire of the Lord again. Learn to stay in constant conversation with God.

CHAPTER 2

FIVE COMMON LIES PEOPLE BELIEVE ABOUT TIME

Letting Truth Set You Free

"A lie is as powerful as the truth, if you believe it."

—Janet Daughtry

It is your beliefs that drive your thoughts. Your thoughts in turn determine your feelings. And it is your feelings that determine your actions.

People do what they do because they believe what they believe. Most people live mainly out of their feelings. But feelings do not always equal truth and feelings do not think.

A lie is as powerful as the truth, if you believe it. To change your behavior, you must know and understand the truth. It is truth that will set you free. To experience victory in any area of your life, you must overcome limiting beliefs in that area. In this book, we are addressing time.

Here are five common lies many people believe about time.

1. My solution is working harder.

One lie many people believe is "I can get more done by working harder." But is this true? I do not think so. Rather, working excessively is a symptom of a slave mentality.

In His death bed message in the Gospel of John, Jesus said, *"I am the vine, you are the branches. He who abides in Me, and I in him, bears much fruit; for without Me you can do nothing." (John 15:5)*

Obviously, Jesus understood the importance of abiding. The word "abide" actually means to live, not just spend some time. So it is vital for each of us to invest time with God to know Him so that we trust Him and can follow Him.

Adrian Rogers used to say, **"Why don't people obey God?** It is because they don't know Him. Knowledge of God leads to trust in God. Trust in God leads to obedience to God. And obedience to God leads to blessings by God."

The tricord of leverage is rest, reflection, and revelation. That is why I place such an emphasis on rest in my life. Think about it. Rest leads to reflection and reflection leads to revelation, inspiration, and illumination. Rest is a place where creative ideas and solutions are birthed. And it is ideas that change the world.

In his outstanding book *You²*, Price Pritchett explains 18 principles for building massive success while expending less effort. One of those principles is "Quit trying harder." In that chapter, Pritchett writes:

> Quantum leaps cannot be achieved through incremental steps or through "more of the same." You've got to shift gears. You have to follow new patterns of thought and action. The rules of what works and what doesn't always change when you are trying to make a move from normal performance to you².

> More of the same usually gets you more of the same... Sooner or later you're going to reach the point where you can't try any harder... Sometimes, in fact, intensifying your efforts produces nothing but bigger problems.

> Now this is not an argument against self-discipline or persistence. Those are true virtues. Over a lifetime they can make a powerful contribution to success and achievement. They are fundamental to the development of your talents. It's extremely important to apply yourself diligently, and sometimes "staying power" is what delivers a big win.

> But ordinarily you will find that trying harder produces only incremental gains, not quantum leaps. Also keep in mind that trying

harder (even a lot harder) sometimes offers little more than a straight path to burnout. Attempting to succeed through "more of the same," being resolute, and relying on committed effort, can blind you to better pathways.

As a 30-60-100 dream coach, I think about leveraging time and quantum leaps. Big dreams take big faith and bring glory to God.

During his Thanksgiving message shared in Culpeper in 2013, Mark Batterson, author of *The Circle Maker*, said "When you pray to God regularly, some irregular things will happen. When you step out in faith, God does some incredible things. If it's not crazy, God's probably not in it. God honors bold prayers because bold prayers honor God."

2. When I go to bed does not matter.

A second lie people often believe is "It does not matter when I go to sleep or when I get up." I disagree strongly. For 20 years, I worked as a "sleep doctor" caring for patients while they slept. I have extensive training and experience to understand the importance of rest and sleep.

I have read that every hour of sleep before midnight is worth three hours of sleep after midnight. Whether this is true or not, I definitely believe God created us to be in synch with His creation. In other words, we are most effective when we get up early before the sun rises and go to bed early, not long after the sun sets.

In his YouTube video "How to Wake Up Early," Robin Sharma describes the value of joining "The 5 AM club" (i.e., getting up at 5 AM each morning). Robin says **the three golden hours are 5-8 AM** because you can often get more done in those three hours than in the rest of the day. He says emphatically, "Win the battle of the bed!" The things that you schedule are the things that get done.

3. I do not need a coach or cannot afford one.

A third common lie many people believe is "I do not need a coach to steward my time well."

If that is the case, let me ask you …

- How is it going with your time and priorities?
- How are your life, your family, your finances, and your health?
- Are you trading your time for money? Is money more valuable to you than your time?
- How much time do you really waste each week? And what are your time wasters?
- If you were to put a value on your time (e.g., $10/hour, $20/hour, $100/hour, or $1,000/hour), how much are your time wasters costing you?
- How much are your lack of clarity and focus costing you?
- When an opportunity presents itself for you to save a lot of time, how do you respond?
- How much is it costing you not to have a coach?

The real question is, "Can you afford NOT to have a coach and, if so, for how long?" A coach provides S.E.A.—Support, Encouragement, and Accountability. Accountability is the password to your future.

"Just as every great athlete has a coach, so does every great life."

Most people live in fear, afraid to change what they are doing to live their lives more fully. That is why I added the chapter "*Conquer Fear*" to this book.

4. I am not wasting much time.

A fourth lie you may believe is "I am not wasting much time every week." In a recent survey I did, I was absolutely shocked at how many of the responders grossly underestimated the number of hours they are wasting every week. It is because they are not aware of what constitutes a time waster or how they are allocating their time.

How much time are you wasting each week? Do you know? What are your regular times wasters? How much are these costing you, financially, emotionally, relationally, and spiritually? To be a good steward with your time, you must develop an awareness of how you are using your time.

5. My clutter is okay.

A fifth lie many people believe is "The clutter in my life and space where I live and work is not costing me dearly." I have certainly been guilty of that. Disorder leads to loss of clarity and less focus. Your home and workspace matter a lot.

In summary, five common lies people believe about time include:

- The solution is working harder.
- When I go to bed does not matter.
- I do not need a coach or cannot afford one.
- I do not have costly time wasters.
- My clutter is okay.

Prayer Power

Father, I praise You as the God of truth. I desire to come into alignment with You and Your ways. Shine the light of Your Word on my path (Psalm 119:105) that I may recognize the lies I believe as true. Then help me humble myself, pray, seek Your face, and turn from wicked ways, so that you will hear from heaven, forgive my sin, and heal me and my family (2 Chronicles 7:14). Amen and hallelujah!

Study Guide

Questions:

Q: What is the tricord of leverage, and to what does it lead?
A: The tricord of leverage is rest, reflection, and revelation. Rest leads to reflection and reflection leads to revelation, inspiration, and illumination.

Q: Why is rest so important to you and to the world?
A: Rest is a place where creative ideas and solutions are birthed. And it is ideas that change the world.

Q: Which of the five lies is hurting you and your effectiveness the most? How is that impacting your life negatively?

_____

_____

Simple Action Step:
Start going to bed by 10:00 p.m. so you can get up at 5:00 a.m., rested and ready to receive God's love and instructions for you.

CHAPTER 3

FIVE SIMPLE STRATEGIES TO STEWARD YOUR TIME

Combining Strategy and Simplicity for Leverage

"The simplest solution is almost always the best one."

Stewardship is the careful and responsible management of something entrusted to one's care. A steward recognizes that he does not own the resources, but rather is appointed to supervise the provision and distribution of those resources.

How you live your life changes dramatically when you realize you do not own anything, but rather it is all on loan from God.

To be a good steward with your time, it is important for you to be aware of these five ways to use your time:

- You can waste your time
- You can spend your time
- You can invest your time
- You can leverage your time
- You can leverage other people's time

Let us take a look now at five simple strategies to be a good steward with your time, including rest, journal, simplify, renew your mind, and focus.

1. Rest

The first strategy to be a good steward with your time is rest. This seems counterintuitive. Society and our flesh nature say you have to work harder to get more done. But I disagree.

Rest leads to reflection, which in turn leads to revelation, inspiration, and illumination. Together, rest, reflection, and revelation form the tricord of leverage. Leverage is being able to accomplish more with less effort.

The most important lesson I have ever learned in my life is this, "To be spiritually healthy, you must ruthlessly eliminate hurry from your life!" That is because love and hurry are incompatible. In the Greatest Commandment, Jesus said the entire Bible can be summarized in one word and that is LOVE.

Then one of them, a lawyer, asked Him a question, testing Him, and saying, "Teacher, which is the great commandment in the law?" Jesus said to him, "'You shall love the LORD your God with all your heart, with all your soul, and with all your mind.' This is the first and great commandment. And the second is like it: 'You shall love your neighbor as yourself.' **On these two commandments hang all the Law and the Prophets.**" *(Matthew 22:35-40)*

2. Journal

A second strategy to steward your time is journaling. For me, **journaling is the key to unlock my dreams**. Why? Here are just a few of the many benefits of journaling.

Journaling helps you slow down. This leads to Rest, Reflection, and Revelation, the tricord of leverage.

Journaling leads to more clarity. Writing things down helps you process and organize your thoughts. It also helps you follow through better. **The greater the clarity you have, the more favor you will experience.**

Journaling allows God to be your Master Coach. And what a great Coach He is. In your devotional time, learn to ask God questions and write down what you hear.

Journaling leads to a greater awareness. It helps you recognize what is working and what is not. As you notice more of what is happening around you, you are able to seize more opportunities.

Journaling allows you to plan better. Failure to plan is a plan to fail. Most people do not plan to fail, but most people fail to plan.

Journaling saves you time. Studies have shown that every minute of planning saves you 10 minutes in implementation. That means investing six minutes of time writing down your goals saves you 60 minutes of time implementing those goals.

Writing down your goals also helps you earn more. A study of Harvard graduates found that after two years, the three percent who had written goals achieved more financially than the other 97% percent combined.

A corollary to that is only three percent of people have written goals. Are you one of those three percent or are you part of the 97% percent crowd that is flailing and achieving much less than they were created to?

*Then the LORD answered me and said: "**Write the vision** and make it plain on tablets, that he may run who reads it. For the vision is yet for an appointed time; But at the end it will speak, and it will not lie. Though it tarries, wait for it; because it will surely come, it will not tarry." (Habakkuk 2:2-3)*

3. Simplify

A third strategy to be a good steward with your time is to simplify. You must "Simplify to multiply." Less really is more. The simplest solution is almost always the best one.

One of the first steps to living your big dreams is to declutter your life and space where you live and work.

In their book *The Knowing—Doing Gap*, Jeffrey Pfeffer and Robert Sutton write: "Simplicity, clarity, and priority are intimately linked. For an organization to maintain a focus on its highest priorities, it must simplify and repeatedly clarify them so that everyone in the organization knows implicitly what to do and what not to do."

For our boasting is this: the testimony of our conscience that we conducted ourselves in the world in simplicity and godly sincerity, not with fleshly wisdom but by the grace of God, and more abundantly toward you. (2 Corinthians 1:12)

4. Renew Your Mind

A fourth strategy to be a good steward with your time is renewing your mind. Let us take a closer look at the importance of your mindset. What you think about is extremely important. It is written, *"For as he thinks in his heart, so is he."* *(Proverbs 23:7)*

When you change your thinking, you change your life. Realize that 99% of the choices you make, you do not make. Your subconscious mind makes those for you. We learn enough trash by the time we are five years old to give us problems for the rest of our lives. Behavioral scientists say that on average we have about 600 negative thoughts go through our mind each day.

So how do you renew your mind and overcome stinking thinking? You must know and understand the truth. The truth will set you free. It is your beliefs that drive your thoughts. Your thoughts in turn drive your emotions, and your emotions drive your actions.

You are the result of all the concepts, ideas, and beliefs you hold as true, whether they are true or not. You are today where your thoughts have brought you. You will be tomorrow where your thoughts take you.

People do what they do because they believe what they believe. Most people live mainly out of their feelings. But feelings do not always equal truth and feelings do not think. **A lie is as powerful as the truth, if you believe it!**

"Do not conform any longer to the pattern of this world, but be transformed by the renewing of your mind" (Romans 12:2)

5. Focus

A fifth strategy to be a good steward with your time is focus. Clarity and focus go hand in hand. Without clarity you cannot have focus. Clarity can be defined as knowing exactly what you want, in measurable and reachable ways that are intensely clear, ultra specific, and totally inspiring to you.

You must know what you want to get it and where you want to go to get there. Imagine going on a trip and not knowing where you want to go. If you want to hit your target, you must know what your target is and where it is. Imagine you are given a bow and arrow to hit a target, but you are blindfolded and do not know what the target is or where it is. What is the likelihood of you hitting the target? It is extremely slim.

Yet, that is how most people live their lives. They give very little thought to who they are and where they want to be. So of course, it is difficult for them to find their sweet spot. The greater the clarity, the greater the favor you will experience, with both God and man.

How do you redeem your time? The key is to focus! The secret is figuring out what it is you want to do and who you want to serve, and then focusing your attention on the steps that will get you there.

Realize that the time you spend you can never get back. If you invest your time toward something else that you make a priority, it is gone forever.

Your family deserves your focus.
Your business deserves your focus.
Your friends deserve your focus.
You deserve your focus!

To love your neighbor fully, you must first love yourself.

The Focusing Question

Let us talk now about The Focusing Question, one of the most important questions you can ask yourself every day. I first learned about this while participating in The Champions Club led by Vic Johnson. The Focusing Question comes from Gary Keller's book *The One Thing: The Surprisingly Simple Truth Behind Extraordinary Results*.

Here is The Focusing Question: **"What is ONE Thing you can do that by doing it everything else will either be easier or unnecessary?"** Asking this question daily and writing down your answer will lead to extraordinary results. That is what I want. How about you?

If you really want to add power to The Focusing Question, then ask the Lord that question and customize it slightly. For example:

Lord, what is ONE thing I can do today (this week, this month, this year) that by doing it everything else will either be easier or unnecessary?

Lord, what is ONE Thing I can do this week (month) for my finances (marriage, health) that by doing it everything else will either be easier or unnecessary?

King David was a man after God's heart because he developed the habit of inquiring of the LORD. *Then King David went in and sat before the LORD; and he said: "Who am I, O Lord GOD? And what is my house, that You have brought me this far?" (2 Samuel 7:18)*

Prayer Power

Father, I praise You as the God of wisdom and understanding (Proverbs 3:19). Help me to understand these five simple strategies to steward my time and then apply them to my life. Help me to rest, journal, simplify, renew my mind, and focus. Take this from head knowledge and burn it into my heart and habits. In Jesus' name I pray. Amen and hallelujah!

Study Guide

Questions:

Q: What are the benefits of simplicity, clarity, and priority?
A: Simplicity, clarity, and priority are intimately linked. For an organization to maintain a focus on its highest priorities, it must simplify and repeatedly clarify them so that everyone in the organization knows implicitly what to do and what not to do.

Q: How do you redeem your time?
A: The key is to focus! The secret is figuring out what it is you want to do and who you want to serve, and then focusing your attention on the steps that will get you there.

Q: What is the Focusing Question?
A: "What is ONE Thing you can do that by doing it everything else will either be easier or unnecessary?"

Simple Action Step:

During your journaling time each morning, ask the Lord the Focusing Question.

CHAPTER 4
TEN BIG TIME WASTERS

Identifying Where You Are Wasting Time

"Let him who would enjoy a good future waste none of his present."
—Roger Babson

Most people do not value their time. While they think they do, a careful observation of their behavior reveals otherwise. Your everyday habits are broadcasting your belief system, your fear, and your unmet needs loud and clear.

As *The Time Doctor*^{TM}, here are 10 big time wasters that I have noticed are common among people:

1. Not living on purpose

By far, the number one time waster for the vast majority of people is not living on purpose.

If your ladder is leaning against the wrong wall, it does not matter how fast you climb that ladder; you will never get to the right place.

Obviously, many people are searching for their purpose because Pastor Rick Warren's book, *The Purpose Driven Life*, sold more than 30 million copies.

To live on purpose, you must know what your purpose is. Discovering your purpose is actually much easier than it seems. The best resource I have found to do that is *The On-Purpose Person*, an outstanding book by my friend Kevin W. McCarthy.

2. Lack of clarity and focus

Clarity and focus go hand in hand. Without clarity (e.g., knowing what you want or where you want to go), you will not have focus. And without focus, you cannot see clearly. Imagine looking through binoculars that are out of focus. Obviously, the image you see will not be clear.

What is clarity? My favorite definition is this: "Clarity is knowing exactly what you want, in measurable and reachable ways that are intensely clear, ultra-specific, and totally inspiring to you."

To hit your target, you must know what your target is and where it is. Imagine you are blindfolded, have a bow and arrow, and someone spins you around in a circle 10 times. The likelihood of you hitting your target is close to zero, especially if you never knew where the target was to start with.

To get to where you want to be, you must know where you are to start with, where you are going, and how to get there. Would you go on a long distance trip to a foreign country without a guide, a map, a GPS, or a plan?

In May 2013, I had the privilege of attending the Chick-fil-A Leadercast in Leesburg, Virginia. The main venue was in Atlanta, Georgia, but the live event was broadcast to many other venues across the United States and world. The theme was "Simply Lead."

Of all the great speakers I heard, Andy Stanley was my favorite. He said, ***"Complexity is the enemy of everything, including clarity!*** The mist of your mind will eventually become a fog in your organization." Understanding this is essential for success because the greater your clarity, the more favor you will experience.

Andy shared that for more than a decade he has carried around a 3×5 index card with **three questions to keep leadership simple: 1) What are we doing? 2) Why are we doing it? 3) Where do I fit in?**

3. Poor planning or no planning

A third big time waster is poor planning or no planning. Failure to plan really is a plan to fail. Most people do not plan to fail, but most people fail to plan. While this seems common sense, it is not common practice because only three percent of people have written goals.

Having a weekly schedule before your week starts helps you be more effective and keep your priorities in order. I believe insufficient time for rest and reflection is often the culprit for poor planning and suboptimal results.

4. Inadequate rest and reflection

I cannot overemphasize the importance of rest to optimize your use of time. You are most creative when you are well rested and relaxed. That is where flow happens in your mind and spirit.

Michael Stay, a close friend and outstanding strategic planner, taught me the tricord of leverage is rest, reflection, and revelation. Why is that? It is because rest leads to reflection and reflection leads to revelation as well as character transformation.

When I journal each morning, the first thing I usually write down is my REST. I write down when I went to sleep, how well I slept, when I got up, and any dreams I remember. Being well rested allows me to function with enthusiasm and at a very high mental state. This allows me to accomplish more when I am working.

5. Overcommitting

Another big time waster is overcommitting, saying yes to too many things. Without a doubt, this dilutes your impact. Failure to keep your commitments disappoints others and yourself. This also takes away the power behind your words. Personally, I want to be great at a few things, not good at many things. What about you?

*But above all, my brethren, do not swear, either by heaven or by earth or with any other oath. But **let your "Yes," be "Yes," and your "No," "No,"** lest you fall into judgment. (James 5:12)*

6. Multitasking

A sixth big time waster is multitasking, also known as switch-tasking. Multiple studies have shown that multitasking almost always results in decreased efficiency. On average, switching tasks leads to a 30% reduction in efficiency. The reason for this is that your mind can only focus on only one task at a time.

7. Checking email frequently

A seventh big time waster is checking and processing email frequently. Would it suffice for you to check your email just at the beginning of your work day and at the end of the day? Would it be okay not to check your email at all for a day or two or maybe an entire weekend? Would the world still turn?

8. Allowing disruptions

An eighth big time waster is allowing disruptions. Having an open door policy, allowing people to call you whenever they want, and checking emails frequently all lead to disruptions.

It is my observation that texting is one of the greatest disruptions in our society today. Why allow someone to barge in on what you are doing right now if what you are doing is truly important? Why is it necessary to respond to a person's text message immediately?

I am not saying do not text and I am not saying do not respond promptly sometimes, but there are many times when you need to be focused and finish what you are working on so that you can move on to the next most important thing.

In America, we live in a culture of instant gratification. However, good leaders model self-control.

9. Quadrant 4 activities

A ninth big time waster is doing Quadrant 4 activities such as watching TV, using Facebook excessively, idle conversations, etc.

In his book "*The Seven Habits of Highly Effective People*," Stephen Covey talked about four quadrants of living—Quadrant 1, 2, 3, and 4.

He drew a square and divided that into two columns and two rows. Over the first column, he put "Urgent." Over the second column, he put "Not Urgent." To the left of the first row, he put "Important." And to the left of the second row, he put "Not Important."

	Urgent	Not Urgent
Important	**I** ACTIVITIES: Crises Putting out fires Pressing problems Deadline-driven projects	**II (Value Quadrant)** Planning, Preparation, Prevention, Empowerment Relationships and Family Sharpen the Saw Service/Community/Church A Big Opportunity Vacations
Not Important	**III** ACTIVITIES: Interuptions Some phone calls Much email Many text messages Some meetings Popular activities	**IV (Time Wasters)** Trivia/busy work Most TV Using Facebook excessively Some phone calls, Most texting Idle conversations Many leisure activities Some email

Quadrant 1 activities are Urgent and Important. They require your immediate attention. Examples are crises, pressing problems, and deadline-driven projects.

When I worked in the operating room, there were many times when things definitely required my immediate attention, but there were also many times when administration staff wanted me to prioritize something that was not urgent. By asking me to do things that were not truly urgent, they compromised the care of patients and the efficiency of the operating rooms.

Quadrant 2 is called the Value Quadrant. This is where you do things that are Important but Not Urgent. This is where you prevent fires instead of having to put them out.

This is where relationships are built, where you make time for recreation, and where new opportunities seem to just drop into your lap.

Quadrant 3 is doing things that are Urgent but Not Important. Nowadays, many of the things people do fit into this category. Examples include interruptions, some phone calls, some emails, some meetings, maybe even most meetings, and popular activities.

Spending too much time in this quadrant can be prevented by having an awareness of why you are doing what you are doing and choosing to invest time to reflect, plan, and figure out how to spend more of your life in Quadrant 2, the Value Quadrant.

Quadrant 4 activities are Not Urgent and Not Important. These are time wasters that yield little value. Some of these activities include watching TV, using Facebook excessively, some phone conversations, etc.

This grid has several applications. Having an awareness of the four quadrants and tracking how you are using your time will help you invest more time in the Value Quadrant.

One way to use the four quadrant model is to take your to-do list each week and to sort all your activities into the various quadrants. Then assess the amount of time you have to accomplish the activities and if necessary, reallocate activities.

A second approach is a one week assessment strategy. Print a copy of the grid for each day of the week and then log in your activities each day. At the end of the week, combine the individual daily data onto one summary grid. Evaluate what you accomplished, how well your time was spent, and whether your workload and commitments need to be reorganized.

The bottom line is "**Do important things first!**"

10. Fear

At the root of most, if not all, procrastination is fear. Most people react instinctively to their fear by running from it, ignoring it, sabotaging their efforts, or quitting their pursuit of the very dream they said they wanted so they will not have to face their fear. To live your big dreams, you must conquer fear! That is why I included an entire chapter in this book about conquering fear.

There is no fear in love; but perfect love casts out fear, because fear involves torment. But he who fears has not been made perfect in love. (1 John 4:18)

In summary, 10 big time wasters are:

- Not living your life and days on purpose
- Lack of clarity and focus
- Poor planning
- Insufficient rest and reflection
- Over-committing
- Multitasking (switch tasking)
- Checking and processing email frequently
- Allowing disruptions
- Quadrant 4 Activities
- Fear

Prayer Power

Father, thank You for this teaching about time wasters. I confess that I have wasted much of my life, but I am at a place where I am ready to live fully for You. Help me to identify and eliminate the time wasters in my life to redeem whatever time I have left on this earth. Teach me to lay up for myself treasures in heaven, where neither moth nor rust destroys and where thieves do not break in and steal (Matthew 6:20). In Jesus' name I pray. Amen and hallelujah!

Study Guide

Questions:

Q: What is the definition of clarity?
A: Clarity is knowing exactly what you want, in measurable and reachable ways that are intensely clear, ultra-specific, and totally inspiring to you.

Q: What is the enemy of clarity?
A: Complexity is the enemy of everything, including clarity.

Q: Of the 10 time wasters listed, which one is the most significant one in your life? What is ONE Thing you can do to eliminate that?

_____
_____
_____
_____

Q: What are the Four Quadrants of living, and which one is the Value Quadrant?
A: Quadrant 1 is Urgent and Important.

Quadrant 2 is Important but Not Urgent.

Quadrant 3 is Urgent but Not Important.

Quadrant 4 is Not Urgent and Not Important.

Quadrant 2 is the Value Quadrant.

Simple Action Step:

Use the four quadrant model by taking your to-do list each week and sorting all your activities into the various quadrants. Then assess the amount of time you have to accomplish the activities and if necessary, reallocate activities.

CHAPTER 5

SACRED TIME—SACRED PLACE

Co-laboring and Co-creating with God

"Every day a miracle comes and every day a miracle goes. Are you expecting it and looking for it?"

—Dr. Oral Roberts

The Story Behind the Story

In mid-December 2010 I received an email from a friend who wrote, "Be expecting a powerful surprise this week! Just remember, in business it's not always about whether you know someone. Often it is about value that was created, or trust that leads to action." A day later, despite five inches of new snow, our mail lady delivered a package containing a leather bound journal titled *Sacred Time—Sacred Place* by Patricia King.

The next morning, I chose to start my day by going to my sacred place (sunroom) to take a close look at this brand new *Sacred Time—Sacred Place* journal. I began my sacred time by reading Patricia King's introduction to this journal. I happened to open the journal to a page stating "In Memory of Oral Roberts!" That immediately grabbed my attention because when I was in Texas a few years earlier, I heard Dr. Mike Murdock tell a fascinating story about Dr. Roberts calling and asking him to write a song in less than an hour containing his death message.

Then I read the key scripture, Song of Solomon 2:14 – *"O my dove, in the clefts of the rock, In the secret pace of the steep pathway, Let me see your form, let me hear your voice; For your voice is sweet, and your form is lovely."*

Next, I read "A Divine Appointment with Oral Roberts." Patricia wrote:

> Three months before Dr. Oral Roberts went to be with the Lord, I had the privilege of being with him in his home. Prior to his departure to glory, he invited a number of ministers from around the world into his private quarters to pray over them. During this time he allowed each to ask a question. I desired to know how he had maintained his devotion time in the midst of many years of leading large mandates and assignments from the Lord. Another guest asked the question before it was my turn and I will never forget his answer.
>
> He called his daily time with the Lord his Sacred Time. He explained that when he went into his prayer closet no one was allowed to interrupt him—including his wife and children. Everyone in his family and ministry respected this sacred time—his time alone with God. No phone calls, no visits, no questions, and today we could say, no internet! He informed us that when God spoke to him in his Sacred Time, he obeyed immediately. He stated, "God never had to speak twice to me. When he spoke, I obeyed." He pursued the Lord with an undivided heart and with full belief that God would speak with him just as He spoke with Moses—face-to-face as a man speaks to his friend.
>
> The enormous fruitfulness of Dr. Oral Roberts' worldwide ministry was clearly a result of the God encounters and visitation of grace he experienced in his uninterrupted and undisturbed Sacred Time and Sacred Place.

Next I read "How to Have a Fruitful Devotional Time with Jesus!" This was so good. I especially liked Patricia's simple teaching about "What do you do in a devotional time?" One of the things that jumped out at me was this, "Make a list of things that distract. Sometimes in the midst of your devotion time you might receive some distracting thoughts such as, 'Oh, I better remember to pay that bill later and email a friend.' Keep a small notepad available, and write those things down so you do not have to think on them again until after your devotion time is over."

Finally, I read her "One Year Bible Reading Plan." Holy Spirit then prompted me to start with Day #1, so I read out loud Genesis 1-2 and Matthew 1 in the Maxwell Leadership Bible declaring and decreeing God's Word. As I read these three chapters in the Bible, Genesis 2:24-25 and Matthew 1:18-25 stood out. These emphasize the importance of unity with your spouse and obedience to God.

I then wrote by hand this two-way prayer as my first entry in my *Sacred Time, Sacred Place* journal:

> Wow Jesus! My spirit is jumping for joy. Thank You for laying out the entire sequence of steps that was necessary to lead my friend to sow this uncommon seed, *Sacred Time—Sacred Place*, into my life. Thank You for this morning's rich abiding time. To You, I give all glory, honor, and praise. Blessed be Your holy name.

> *Thank You Joseph for your obedience. Your past has not been wasted. Your choices and decisions have led you to this turning point. Today, I lay before you life and death, blessings and curses. Therefore, CHOOSE LIFE. Choose Me.* **What you were missing was your sacred place.** *Even your sacred time was not sacred. Today you begin a new life in Me, with Me, and through Me. Today you move from the natural to the supernatural.*

> *Delight yourself in Me and I will give you the desires of your heart. What are your desires?*

> Thank you for asking Jesus!

> 1. I'd like to be debt free by December 31, 2010.

> 2. I'd like to launch the 30-60-100 Master's Mind Coaching™ by Christmas (2010).

> 3. I'd like to be praying and decreeing financial blessings with Julia starting today.

> *Ok, Joseph. I've heard your prayers and heart cry. BE blessed.*

It is interesting how God answered the first prayer so quickly. Just one week later at Christmas, my wife and I received a gift wiping out more than

$100,000 of our debt. Five months after that, God stirred someone's heart to completely eliminate our remaining $100,000 of debt in a single day. That is amazing.

The Importance of Sacred Time and Sacred Place

When someone tells me, "I am not a morning person," I cringe on the inside. That is because I know God wants us to be in synch with His creation. And how you start your day has a big impact on how the day works out.

Throughout history, God has accomplished great things through people surrendered to Him and who knew how to hear His voice.

Moses had a sacred place. He called it his "tent of meeting." It was a place where he met face-to-face with God and God spoke to him as a man speaks to his friend. (Exodus 33:7-11)

In the 1500's, Martin Luther ignited the entire Protestant Reformation. He was so busy he invested at least four hours daily praying and meeting with God to get his work done.

In the 1930's, Frank Laubach invested two years of his life practicing the presence of God every 15 to 30 minutes. As a result of that habit, in the last 40 years of his life, Laubach developed the Each One Teach One literacy campaign, used to teach 60 million people to read in their own language, all across the globe. He wrote over 50 books and became an international presence in literacy, religious, and governmental circles—having an influence on poverty, injustice, and illiteracy worldwide. His influence spread to presidents as well as across the underdeveloped areas of the world.

Dr. Yonghi Cho pastors a church in Seoul Korea with more than one million members. His secret to success was investing five hours each morning in his sacred place on his knees praying and seeking God's face.

After years of establishing the Walk Through the Bible ministry globally, Dr. Bruce Wilkinson found himself burned out. In his book *Secrets of the Vine*, he shares the secret to his turnaround and great fruitfulness was three simple daily habits, all associated with his sacred time and sacred place.

Simple Keys to Powerful Devotional Times

What you do in your devotional time and the order you do it will be unique to you. Find a routine that you feel comfortable with and that works well for you and then stick to it.

1. Establish your sacred time and sacred place

The first key to having powerful devotional times is to decide on a sacred time and sacred place, a set time and a set place where you will meet with God. Then you need to keep those sacred every day. To me, the term "sacred time" seems much more significant than quiet time or devotional time, so I prefer the former.

Give God the first fruits of your time, the first and best of your time, not the leftovers. If you believe your most important meeting of the day is your meeting with God, you will make this a high priority. Remember, good habits are the key to all success and successful people do daily what unsuccessful people do occasionally.

If you do not allot ample time (e.g., at least 30 minutes) to meet with God daily, I can assure you He is not your first love. You can say He is, but love is spelled T.I.M.E. Getting to know God intimately takes time.

Ideally, your sacred place is somewhere where there are no or few distractions, allowing you to keep your focus on God. For many people, having access to the internet or a Smart phone may easily distract them.

God's promise to you in Psalm 91:1 is this, *"He who dwells in the secret place of the Most High shall abide under the shadow of the Almighty."*

2. Commit yourself and your time to the Lord

A second key to powerful devotional times is to commit yourself and your time to the Lord. It is my practice when I first go to my sacred place for my sacred time, to kneel down for a few minutes to pray. Usually, I start by saying the Lord's Prayer in a personalized way, committing my meeting, day, and agenda to God. I give God permission to rearrange my schedule as He sees fit. I invite Holy Spirit to lead and guide me in my devotional time.

3. Journal

It is my habit to journal early during my sacred time. I do that to capture inspired thoughts God has already given me that morning as well as to thank God and write down what He is saying to me. After years of journaling hours per day, I have found this habit is the one that ushers me into the presence of God the fastest. Then when I read the Bible or something else, my spirit is ready to receive what the Lord wants me to know.

When you journal, I personally recommend starting by thanking Jesus for things and circumstances within the previous 24 hours. That creates an attitude of gratitude and prepares you to listen to God. Then invite the Lord to speak to you, expecting He will. Hearing God's voice is easier than most people think.

"My sheep hear My voice, and I know them, and they follow Me." (John 10:27)

There is a protocol for entering the presence of the King and that includes thanksgiving and praise. Psalm 100:4 states, *"Enter into His gates with thanksgiving, And into His courts with praise. Be thankful to Him, and bless His name."* After thanking God, it is important to praise Him in some manner to enter His presence. Many people like to do this by listening to worship songs.

In addition to helping you hear God more clearly, journaling helps organize your thoughts as you write things down. Your journal entries also bring encouragement. When you start to journal, you will find it encouraging to re-read journal entries from the previous day and week. Your faith and trust in God will grow as you refine this wonderful habit.

My chapter "Uncommon Journaling For Divine Destiny" explains a lot more about journaling and how to hear God's voice through journaling.

4. Read the Bible

Obviously, the best way to know God is by reading or listening to the Bible. That is because Jesus is the Word of God. The Bible serves as the gold standard or plumb line for truth.

In the beginning was the Word, and the Word was with God, and the Word was God. He was in the beginning with God. All things were made through Him, and without Him nothing was made that was made. In Him was life, and the life was the light of men... And the Word became flesh and dwelt among us, and we beheld His glory, the glory as of the only begotten of the Father, full of grace and truth. (John 1:1-4, 14)

It is beneficial to read the Bible out loud and even make decrees of God's promises because there is tremendous power in the spoken Word. According to Romans 10:17, *"faith comes by hearing, and hearing by the word of God."*

5. Pray

Prayer is simply talking to God and listening to Him. Ideally, it is a two-way conversation, not a monologue. You need to be quiet in order to listen to God.

During the first few years after I began journaling, the Lord told me several times, "When you learn to listen to Me, you will learn to listen to people." So my question to you is "How well do you listen to God?"

Journaling is a simple way to record your stream of consciousness while focused on God. For those who believe in praying in tongues, this is a powerful tool and habit.

6. Make a list of things that distract you

Keep a paper handy during your devotional time to write down thoughts that come to your mind that distract you from focusing on God. For example, you might think "I need to pay that bill later today" or "I have to call so-and-so this morning." Writing those thoughts down helps you to stop thinking about them.

Let us review simple keys to powerful devotional times:

- Establish your sacred time and sacred place
- Commit yourself and your time to the Lord
- Journal
- Read the Bible
- Pray
- Make a list of things that distract you

Words from Jesus (WFJ)

To help you better understand God's perspective on our sacred time and sacred place, let me share these inspired and encouraging journal entries written by hand during my sacred time in my sacred place while facilitating the *I Was Busy, Now I'm Not*™ coaching program.

> *Joseph, thank you for choosing to invest this time together this morning.* ***This is your most important meeting of the day.*** *Do not listen to anyone who tells you otherwise. This is the place where you receive your marching orders for your day.* ***This is your first fruits offering to Me.*** *I want your first fruits, not your leftovers. I want the best you have to offer, so I can give you My best and multiply what you have. Seeking My kingdom and My righteousness starts with your sacred time and sacred place. Do not let anyone convince you otherwise. (March 6, 2014)*

> *Joseph, thank you for choosing to invest the first and best portion of your time with Me and to record our journey together. I AM excited about what is happening in your life. I AM glad to see you bearing so much fruit because that brings glory to our Father. You are merciful, so you have been shown mercy. You exist to serve by inspiring love. You are manifesting that. That is what Rick and Joey Saunders, Gary Beaton, and Barbara and Rich Freeman are saying to you. They are experiencing My love in ways they never have before.* ***You are intimately connected to the Dream Giver and that allows you to believe in other people's dreams.*** *Your breakthrough has happened. Your confidence is soaring. People recognize your gifts and are willing to invest in you at a high level. Be blessed. (March 20, 2014)*

> *Joseph, thank you for making this meeting with me your most important meeting of the day. You have won the battle with your sacred place and sacred time. This is now a habit that you long for.* ***It is in the "secret place," as I say in Psalm 91, that you receive full protection against attacks of the enemy.*** *It is in this place that you receive the clarity to know what you should do each day and how to start your days. It is here where you experience Me in extraordinary ways. Our meeting together is the game plan, the strategy to live each day to the fullest. You are in a place of much growth. You are in a place in your life where you are listening well. My sheep hear My voice. I know them and they follow Me. You live this and can pass this onto others. Rejoice*

and be exceedingly glad. I love you with an everlasting love. Be blessed. (March 21, 2014)

Thank you Joseph for choosing to invest your first fruits of time with Me to help you get your day off to a good start. As your influence grows, so will the demands on your life. I have you teaching the I Was Busy, Now I'm Not™ coaching program month after month to remind you of what is important to steward your time. You have been taking massive action, but you must never forget to let your yes be yes. **How you keep your sacred time and sacred place is the best indicator of how busy you are. This is your most important daily habit.** *Another important indicator is keeping the Sabbath holy. And a third habit is daily exercise. Learn to say no much more often. You can help people the most by coaching them, even if only one session. You do not have to do the work for them. (March 27, 2014)*

Thank you Joseph for choosing to listen, trust, and obey Me, for choosing to keep your sacred time and sacred place sacred. This past week has been one of your most profound weeks of your life in terms of fruitfulness. You have become a miracle to so many other people and now it is time for people to be miracles to you. As Cheryl-Ann saw in her vision, **you have been casting out seeds of good will into the ocean and now a tidal wave of blessings is coming back into your life and family.** *Your parents, your children, your extended family, and your friends will all see, will all witness that your faithfulness to Me has paid off in extraordinary ways. I AM the way, the truth, and the life. I AM the gate. Your understanding of Me and My ways is going to a whole new level. You will reconcile the breeches that have taken place in your life this year. My truth will set you free. I AM truth. I AM light. I AM your guiding star. I love with an everlasting love. Be blessed. (March 30, 2014)*

Joseph, thank you for choosing to still yourself, fix your eyes on Me, tune to spontaneity, and journal. Those are the four keys to hearing My Voice. My sheep hear My voice. I know them and they follow Me. You can apply these keys any time throughout your day. That is why **the 60-60 Experiment is so powerful because you connect with Me at regular intervals during the day.** *This morning I want you to read Practicing His Presence, Psalm 139, Psalm 91, and Psalm 1. Understand what it means to abide in Me. That is the key to fruitfulness. That is the key to prospering in all areas of your life. Because you are showing mercy to others, I will show mercy to you.*

Know that you My brother are richly blessed and highly favored. I have created you to inspire love in others. I have created you to draw others to Me through your love. (March 31, 2014)

Joseph, thank you for choosing to invest the first fruits of your time with Me! I delight in this time we have together. I AM thankful for your choice to slow down, be still, and listen. I AM Jehovah, the living and true God, the resurrected Savior. I AM the Source of true power and everlasting life. I AM the Word made flesh among you. My Spirit dwells within you. You are eternal. You are a spirit in a body, not vice versa. **Feed your spirit and your body will be nourished too.** *Receive all that I AM today. Be all that I AM today. Let My glory shine forth through you today. You are blessed to be a blessing. I declare that so. You are richly blessed and highly favored. Soak in My presence. Bask in My glory. The glory of the Lord God Almighty is upon you. Behold My glory. (April 2, 2014)*

Joseph, thank you for choosing to invest the first fruits of your time with Me this morning! This is time well spent. **This is the best way to leverage your time.** *Little by little, this habit is being engrained into who you are. You are realizing the significance of keeping your sacred time and sacred place sacred. Dr. Oral Roberts had people he delegated the tasks and projects to. You must do likewise. (April 7, 2014)*

Joseph, thank you for choosing to take the time out in your day to commune with Me! **This sacred time and sacred place is where you get the most clarity. Trust Me with your provision.** *I know what you need. I AM sending great wealth for you to manage and distribute. You have a keen heart to meet the needs of those who will grow My kingdom. Behold and watch the glory of the Lord. Thank you for your faithfulness. Be blessed. (April 10, 2014)*

Make God Your Dream Partner

Starting in the last quarter of 2013, I began developing more focus and clarity than ever before in my life. Two new habits contributed to this. One is my habit of journaling by hand during my sacred time in my sacred place. And the other is asking this Focusing Question:

"LORD, what is one thing I can do today that by doing it everything else will be easier or unnecessary?"

I encourage you to ask God that question each morning and write down in a journal what you hear. I think you will be amazed at what happens.

As Dr. Mike Murdock wrote in his "Morning Motivation" on January 10, 2014:

Make God your dream partner. Let God decide your daily agenda and your dream will be achieved.

A God-inspired dream will always require the participation of God. One hour with God could easily reveal to you the fatal flaws in your most carefully laid plans. He who succeeds in prayer succeeds.

Develop conversation ability in the presence of God. Holy Spirit responds to words. Talking aloud to God creates profound and indescribable results.

Prayer Power

Father God, more than anything else you desire an intimate relationship with Your children. I acknowledge that my most important meeting every day is my meeting with You. Help me to prioritize my sacred time and sacred place in such a way that I will experience You in extraordinary ways for extraordinary fruit. It is my heart's desire to seek You and find You (Jeremiah 29:13). Like Abraham, Moses, King David, the apostle Paul, Martin Luther, Brother Lawrence, and Frank Laubach, I want to be Your friend. In Jesus' name I pray. Amen and hallelujah!

Study Guide

Questions

Q: What did Dr. Oral Roberts say was the key to the enormous fruitfulness of his world-wide ministry?
A: Dr. Oral Roberts attributed his enormous fruitfulness to his sacred time and sacred place and the God encounters he experienced there. When God spoke to him in his sacred time, he obeyed immediately. God never had to speak to him twice.

Q: What is the first and most important key to powerful devotional times?
A: Establishing your sacred time and sacred place and then keeping those sacred.

Simple Action Step:

Make a commitment to keep you sacred time and sacred place sacred. Then keep track each week how many days you succeed at that.

CHAPTER 6
APPLYING THE POWER OF LESS

Priorities and Habits to Put First Things First

"Be the change that you wish to see in the world."
—**Mahatma Gandhi**

In the summer of 1998 I read *First Things First* by Stephen Covey. That book dramatically changed my thinking, which led to big changes in my life. That is the book that gave me the courage to step away from my bread-and-butter job when circumstances became unbearable.

In that book, Covey tells a story about a college professor who was teaching a time management course. During one of his classes, he taught a very important life lesson.

The professor set a big glass jar on the table. Next to that he placed some big rocks. The professor asked his students to estimate how many of the big rocks would fit into the jar and to write that down. He then placed the rocks into the jar one at a time until the rocks were up to the top of the jar. When he asked the students if the jar was full, they all said yes.

Then he placed some smaller rocks next to the jar. Once again, he asked the students to guess how many of the small rocks would fit into the jar. The college professor carefully filled the jar with the small rocks one at a time until the last one was up to the top. Once again he asked if the jar was full. This time half the students said yes and half said no.

Then he took some sand and poured that into the jar. Finally, he took some water and poured that into the jar. This time the jar was truly full.

The professor then asked the students why he had done this demonstration for them. What lesson did he want them to learn? One of the students proudly raised his hand and said, "If we are efficient, we can always get more things done."

The professor responded emphatically "No! The big rocks represent the important things in your life. If you do not put them in your jar of life first, either they will not fit, or else when they go in they will make a big mess."

In the year 2000, God dumped over my jar of life and gave me a second chance to start all over. This time I chose to put in the most important rock first—Jesus. My marriage, my family, my business, and everything else are all now built on that.

When you ask Christians what their top priorities are, many say "God, family, church, and work" in that order. But if you look at how those people spend their time and money that just is not true for many of them.

Steve and Tara Connell say, "Do not tell me what is important to you. Show me how you live and I will tell you what is important to you. Your pocketbook and your calendar reveal where your heart is."

I believe a godly order of priorities is "God first, your spouse second, your children third (if you have children), and your work and church next. Your spouse is to be a higher priority than your children, and your work is at least as important as going to church.

Biblical Wisdom about the Most Important Priority

God not only wants to be first in your life; He wants to be the center of your life, around which everything else revolves. According to Gary Keller, author of *The ONE Thing*, "priority" actually comes from a Latin word meaning "first." The word remained singular (i.e., priority, not priorities) until the 1900's when the meaning morphed to "something that matters."

*And God spoke all these words, saying: "I am the LORD your God, who brought you out of the land of Egypt, out of the house of bondage. **You shall have no other gods before Me.** You shall not make for yourself a carved image, or any likeness of anything that is in heaven above, or that is in the earth beneath, or that is in the water under the earth; you shall not bow down to them nor serve them. For I, the LORD your God, am a jealous God, visiting the iniquity of the fathers on the* *children to the third and fourth generations of those who hate Me, but showing mercy to thousands, to those who love Me and keep My commandments." (Exodus 20:1-6)*

When asked "which is the great commandment," **Jesus summed up the entire Bible in one word—LOVE.**

Then one of them, a lawyer, asked Him a question, testing Him, and saying, "Teacher, which is the great commandment in the law?" Jesus said to him, "'You shall love the LORD your God with all your heart, with all your soul, and with all your mind.' This is the first and great commandment. And the second is like it: 'You shall love your neighbor as yourself.' On these two commandments hang all the Law and the Prophets." (Matthew 22:35-40)

Love is spelled T-I-M-E. When you love someone, you think about them and want to spend time with them. You love God by investing time with Him, prioritizing Him, and getting to know Him by meditating on His Word. You love your spouse by investing time with her/him and prioritizing her/him. You love your neighbor by investing time with her/him, listening, and being in the moment.

And, what is love? Here I am talking about "agape" (divine or unconditional love). According to Josh McDowell, **love protects and provides**. Josh is a leading Christian apologist, evangelist, and writer, having authored or co-authored about 115 books, including *Evidence That Demands a Verdict*, *More Than a Carpenter*, *A Ready Defense*, and *Right from Wrong*.

According to the "love chapter" in the Bible, love is patient and kind.

"Love suffers long (is patient) and is kind; love does not envy; love does not parade itself, is not puffed up; does not behave rudely, does not seek its own, is not provoked, thinks no evil; does not rejoice in iniquity, but rejoices in the truth; bears all things, believes all things, hopes all things, endures all things." (1 Corinthians 13:4-7)

To stay full of love so you can pour love into others, it is vital to guard your heart and your motives. *Keep your heart with all diligence, for out of it spring the issues of life. (Proverbs 4:23)*

Humility is also essential to love as God loves us. John the Baptist said, *"He must increase, but I must decrease" (John 3:30).* And Proverbs

22:4 teaches, *"By humility and the fear of the LORD are riches and honor and life."*

The Importance of Habits

> *"Good habits are the key to all success!"*
> **—Og Mandino**

Next to the Bible, the book that had the greatest impact on my life was *The Greatest Salesman in the World* by Og Mandino. An excerpt from Scroll #1 of this book states:

> In truth, the only difference between those who fail and those who succeed lies in the difference of their habits. **Good habits are the key to success. Bad habits are the unlocked door to failure.** Thus, the first law I will obey, which precedes all others is—I will form good habits and become their slave.
>
> When I was a child, I was slave to my impulses; now I am slave to my habits, as are all grown men. I have surrendered my free will to the years of accumulated habits and the past deeds of my life have already marked out a path which threatens to imprison my future. My actions are ruled by appetite, passion, prejudice, greed, love, fear, environment, habit, and the worst of these tyrants is habit.
>
> Therefore, if I must be a slave to habit, let me be a slave to good habits. My bad habits must be destroyed and new furrows prepared for good seed. I will form good habits and become their slave.

Dr. Mike Murdock, founder of *The Wisdom Center*, teaches, "The secret of your future is hidden in your daily routine. Successful people do daily what unsuccessful people do occasionally." Just look at world class athletes. They achieve great things because of daily disciplines and coaching.

How do you form long-lasting habits? The best way is by applying the power of less. Focus on one habit at a time, one month at a time, so that you will be able to focus all your energy on creating that one habit. Imagine what your life might look like a year from now if you establish one new habit each month for the next 12 months. You will grow so much your friends may not even recognize you.

What are three simple daily habits to transform your life? In his book *Secrets of the Vine*, Dr. Bruce Wilkinson talks about these three habits that profoundly increased the fruitfulness of his life.

1. Get up early each morning to read the Bible
   (for Dr. Wilkinson, it is 5 a.m.)
2. Write a full page in a daily spiritual journal
   (Keep a gratitude journal daily)
3. Learn to pray and seek God until you find Him

Biblical Wisdom about the Most Important Habits

The Bible describes four habits that will help you live a rich life to be all and do all God intended—Meditate on God's Word, Abide in Jesus, Praise the LORD, and Teach.

1. Meditate on God's Word morning (day) and night

Before Joshua led two million people into the Promised Land, God commanded, ***"This Book of the Law shall not depart from your mouth, but you shall meditate in it day and night,*** *that you may observe to do according to all that is written in it. For then you will make your way prosperous, and then you will have good success. Have I not commanded you? Be strong and of good courage; do not be afraid, nor be dismayed, for the LORD your God is with you wherever you go."* (Joshua 1:8-9)

Before you can lead a multitude into their Promised Land, you must follow Joshua's example—meditating on God's Word morning and night. A leader must lead by example and raise the bar for others to follow. There are no short cuts. There are no other alternative routes.

What about King David? What made him a man after God's own heart? The answer lies in the first three verses of the very first Psalm of the 150 Psalms. In Psalm 1:1-3, God says:

Blessed is the man who walks not in the counsel of the ungodly, nor stands in the path of sinners, nor sits in the seat of the scornful; But his delight is in the law of the LORD, and in His law he meditates day and night. He shall be like a tree planted by the rivers of water that brings forth its fruit in its season, whose leaf also shall not wither; and whatever he does shall prosper.

So, let me ask you, "What does it mean to meditate on God's Word morning and night? On a scale of 1-10, how would you rate your success at this habit?"

2. Abide

In his death bed message after the Last Supper, Jesus told his twelve disciples, *"I am the vine, you are the branches.* **He who abides in Me, and I in him, bears much fruit***; for without Me you can do nothing. If anyone does not abide in Me, he is cast out as a branch and is withered; and they gather them and throw them into the fire, and they are burned. If you abide in Me, and My words abide in you, you will ask what you desire, and it shall be done for you. By this My Father is glorified, that you bear much fruit; so you will be My disciples." (John 15:5-8)*

He who dwells in the secret place of the Most High shall abide under the shadow of the Almighty. (Psalm 91:1)

3. Praise the LORD

The last five Psalms in the Bible all begin and end with "Praise the LORD." Obviously, God put His exclamation point on this important habit in closing out the book of Psalms. Why? **Praise is the prayer that changes everything**. Incidentally, "hallelujah" is a Hebrew word that means "praise the LORD."

Praise the LORD! Praise God in His sanctuary; Praise Him in His mighty firmament! Praise Him for His mighty acts; Praise Him according to His excellent greatness! Praise Him with the sound of the trumpet; Praise Him with the lute and harp! Praise Him with the timbrel and dance; Praise Him with stringed instruments and flutes! Praise Him with loud cymbals; Praise Him with clashing cymbals! Let everything that has breath praise the LORD. Praise the LORD! (Psalm 150:1-6)

4. Teach (i.e., Make disciples who make disciples who make disciples)

"You shall love the LORD your God with all your heart, with all your soul, and with all your strength. And these words which I command you today shall be in your heart. **You shall teach them _diligently_ to your children***, and shall talk of them when you sit in your house, when you walk by the way, when you lie down, and when you rise up. You shall bind them as a sign on your hand, and they shall be as frontlets between your eyes. You shall write them on the doorposts of your house and on your gates." (Deuteronomy 6:5-9)*

God's desired method of teaching is by the parents—not public schools, private schools, or Sunday or Sabbath schools.

In the Great Commission, Jesus commands us to disciple nations, not just people: *"Go therefore and **make disciples of all the nations**, baptizing them in the name of the Father and of the Son and of the Holy Spirit, teaching them to observe all things that I have commanded you; and lo, I am with you always, even to the end of the age." Amen. (Matthew 28:19-20)*

The Importance of Margin

What is Margin? Margin is the space between your current situation or performance and your limits. Margin is a buffer or gap, a place of reserve for reflecting, relating, recharging your batteries, and focusing on the things that matter most. Having more margin usually leads to better choices. Margin creates resiliency. **Contentment, simplicity, balance, and rest lead to margin** and overall better health.

Lack of margin leads to stress, which has a compounding effect. If you are working 12 hour days, seven days a week, you have little margin for anything or anyone who is not already in your schedule. So if anything out of the ordinary happens or if a special opportunity presents itself, you have little capacity to respond to it. If God wants to drop a miracle in your life, you do not have room to receive it.

In his book *Margin: Restoring Emotional, Physical, Financial, and Time Reserves to Overloaded Lives*, Richard Swenson, M.D., says life in modern day America is essentially devoid of time and space. Chronic overloading is the culprit. Margin is the cure. Overload leads to busyness, fatigue, anxiety, and insecurity, whereas margin leads to enjoyment, energy, calm, and security.

There are six key areas you need margin:

- Scheduling: too close together = chaos
- Leadership: need enough credibility to make mistakes and not lose influence
- Financially: living pay day to pay day with no room for error
- Physically: health and weight

- Spiritually: one assignment to the next and not fulfilling God's purpose for your life
- Relationships: Love is spelled T.I.M.E.

The key question for you today is, "How much margin do I really have in these key areas of my life? Or am I just too busy?" BUSY is an acronym for "Burdened Under Satan's Yoke." In John 10:10, Jesus says, *"The thief does not come except to steal, and to kill, and to destroy. I have come that they may have life, and that they may have it more abundantly."* It is up to you to not get in His way through a habit of busyness.

10 Ways to Create Time Margin

OK, so you realize having margin is important, but how do you fit more into an already busy schedule? Sometimes it helps to see things from a different perspective. The following tips to create time margin come from Ron Edmonson in his January 10, 2009 blog post:

1. Put God first. It's amazing in my week and day if I start the day talking to God about my day. If I ask God for margin in my time and to help me complete my "to do" list, He actually seems to listen and help me. (Try it!)
2. Prioritize your life. It is important to have a life purpose. What do you value most? Without knowing this we find ourselves chasing after many things that have little value.
3. Make sure your priorities line up with your desires. That sounds like a contradiction in terms, but it is not. Many times, we say our purpose is one thing, but what we actually do is something entirely different. That is often because people are going to do what people want to do. We may need to ask God to change our heart and plant in us His desires.
4. Stop unnecessary time-wasters. If you "veg" out every night on 3+ hours of television or surfing the net, don't be surprised that you didn't get a blog post written or spend quality time with your children. Most of us form bad habits or have unorganized methods of doing something that waste bulks of our time. Make a list of what you spend the most time doing and see if there are places you can cut. (I suspect there will be.)
5. Work smarter. I can't imagine being successful and leading a team without some system of calendaring your week or keeping a planner, yet I know so many pastors and other ministers who simply handle things as they come up rather than work with a plan. The benefit of organization

is that you can do what you need to do more efficiently and faster and be more productive.

6. Schedule times to organize. This is so important, but most people don't do it. Spending an hour or two actually planning the week will make the whole week more productive. Usually for me this is the first part of my week. If I know where I'm headed and my work space is organized for efficiency, it's much easier to get everything done and still handle distractions, which are sure to come.

7. Do the most necessary things first. You may have tried the A/B/C list of scheduling priorities. It doesn't matter what system you use, but the important thing is that you have one and use it to help your rate of completion.

8. Don't say yes to everything. Be picky with your time allotment based again on your end priorities and goals.

9. Schedule down time. Especially when my boys were younger, I would write on my calendar time for them. That may sound mechanical, but it allows you to be there and keeps things and others from filling up your schedule.

10. Evaluate your schedule often. Plans should not be implemented and then ignored. Develop your plan to create margin in your life, then periodically review the plan to see how you are doing and what needs to be changed.

Balance

I have heard some people say that having balance is important to our overall well-being and others say it is impossible to achieve balance. As a well-trained leadership coach, I know we can only effectively grow in two or three areas of our lives at one time.

One of my favorite messages about balance comes from Brian Klemmer in his book *If How-To's Were Enough We Would All Be Skinny, Rich, and Happy*. In that Brian writes, "Focus is a key to results and is often perceived as a contradiction to balance, but that does not have to be so. **Balance is the key to maintaining power and long term peace of mind. Balance and focus together produce maximum results.**"

Brian discusses the notion that you and I are like squares with four sides—physical, emotional, mental, and spiritual. What makes a square a square is that all four sides are equal. That represents balance. However, because of family, societal, work, and other influences, we often do not develop equally on all four sides.

Rate yourself from a 0 to 10 in each of these four areas to see how balanced you are. A 10 physically means your weight is ideal, you eat healthy, exercise regularly, have normal blood pressure, and no diseases. A 10 emotionally means you can clearly expresses a wide range of appropriate feelings at any time, you are well understood, etc. A 10 mentally means you are smart, read a lot, eager to learn, and have an income that supports your dreams and goals. A 10 spiritually means you have a wonderful relationship with your Creator, manifest the fruit of the Spirit (Galations 5:22-23), and are good at applying Biblical principles to your life.

Prayer Power

Daddy, I praise You as a good God, as a great God. I confess that I have let many things get in the way of my relationship with You. I confess that I have made many mistakes in my life and repent. I want You to be my First Love, the top priority in my life. Help me to do that. I surrender all that I am, all that I have, and all that I want to You and lay that at the foot of the cross. Remove anything that does not belong and add whatever I need. Then bless that and return it to me to be multiplied by Your grace and Your love. In Jesus' name I pray. Amen and hallelujah!

Study Guide

Questions:

Q: What do the "big rocks" represent in your life?
A: The big rocks represent the important things in your life. If you do not put them in your jar of life first, either they will not fit or else they when they go in they will make a big mess.

Q: Do your calendar and checkbook reflect your desired priorities in real terms? If not, what simple change can you make to move toward that goal?
A: _____

_____

_____

_____

_____

_____

Q: How do you form long-lasting habits?
A: The best way is by applying the power of less. Focus on one habit at a time, one month at a time, so that you will be able to focus all your energy on creating that one habit.

Q: How close to the edge are you living your life? How much margin do you have? If you lack margin, what is ONE Thing you can do that by doing it everything else will be easier of unnecessary?
A: _____

_____

_____

_____

_____

_____

Simple Action Step:

Write down three new habits you want to form in the next three months that will have a major impact on your life. Prioritize them. Then for the next three months, focus on establishing one of those habits each month.

CHAPTER 7

DEVELOPING YOUR
ONE YEAR GROWTH CALENDAR

Planning to Succeed

"If you do not control your calendar, it will control you."
—Nelson Searcy

In late 2010 or early 2011, my pastor, Matt Gregory, enrolled in an outstanding, year-long, virtual group coaching program with Nelson Searcy. Nelson is the founder of Church Leader Insights, maximizing pastors and church leaders.

In May 2011, Matt shared with me one of Nelson's audio teachings titled "Developing Your One Year Growth Calendar." That is one of the best messages I have ever heard on the subject of personal growth, so I want to share that with you. In that teaching, Nelson has a conversation with Roy Mansfield.

Nelson starts out by asking this very powerful question: "**What is your intentional plan for personal growth?**"

Years ago when Nelson was first asked that question by a pastor, he answered "Pray hard, go to church, and trust God." Then Nelson realized he did not really have a written, intentional plan for personal growth.

In response, the pastor said something very striking to Nelson: "Well, I can just about guess how much God is going to use you." Nelson took that comment very seriously, realizing if God was going to use him at the next level, he had to go to the next level.

When Nelson first started *The Journey* (Church) in 2002, he knew he was not the pastor he needed to be to lead the church. So he prayed to God almost every day, "God make me into the person I need to be to lead this church at the next level."

The truth for most of us is growth does not happen by accident. Growth does not happen by osmosis, just by hanging out with growing leaders or hoping we can grow.

Growth Must Be Intentional

Most of us need a workable system that we can put together that is going to help us grow. We need a plan (i.e., calendar) of what our growth is going to be like over the next 365 days. This is worth a day of your time to plan the next 364 days of your year.

Just imagine what your life can be like. Imagine what growth can do for you. If you are intentional about going to the next level with your personal growth, some of the dreams that you have been hoping for will start becoming reality.

This idea of personal growth is so important and we all need a system. To get the most out of this process, you need not only an open mind to what is being shared, but you also need a calendar, some paper, and a pen in front of you. If you do not have all those, go and get them now.

Instead of just drifting and wasting your time, you can really move forward if you just have a plan. It is often possible to make up in learning what you lack in natural ability. Choose to enjoy the process of growth as much as the result of growth.

Three Truths about Personal Growth

1. Personal growth is necessary for spiritual growth!

Personal growth and spiritual growth are connected. Personal growth is really a subcategory of spiritual growth. They are not disconnected; they are not two different things. Personal growth is a part of a much larger area of your life that encompasses your whole spiritual being.

The way you manage time, the way you delegate responsibilities, and the way you learn to communicate are all part of spiritual growth. Many Christians understand that all growth is spiritual growth because you are a spirit being with a body and soul, not the other way around. Part of any good spiritual growth plan includes personal growth. But, a lot of leaders miss this.

God calls you to be both faithful and fruitful. If you do not really believe that, you are not going to use every ounce of your energy to pursue growth in every area of your life and will not attain all that God desires.

2. Personal growth requires a plan!

To grow intentionally, you need a plan, a process to work. You need some tracks to grow on, as well as to go on. This personal growth plan is very important. Growth does not happen by accident.

A good idea rarely sneaks up on you. You have to go looking for it. That is what Jesus meant when He said: *"Ask and it will be given to you; seek, and you will find; knock and it will be opened to you." (Matthew 7:7)*

You have been drawn to this teaching today for an exciting reason. Proverbs 16:9 says, *"A man's heart plans his way, but the LORD directs his steps."* That means your responsibility is to come up with the plan and God's responsibility is to determine the outcome.

When putting together a plan, search for new ideas and learn new skills to take you to the next level. When our mind is stretched by a new idea, it never regains its original size or shape. A good plan will help you stretch your mind.

3. Personal growth precedes organizational growth.

Growing organizations are led by growing leaders. According to Dr. John Maxwell's Law of the Lid, "Leadership ability determines a person's level of effectiveness."

Leaders who are not growing limit the potential of their staff and organization. Whenever you see an organization that is growing on a solid foundation and doing great things, you can be sure the leaders in that organization are growing. If you are the same leader you were a year ago, it is likely your job and your organization are the same.

Part of God's plan for growing your organization is to grow you. Throughout the Bible, we see examples of people who were continually growing because they were committed to their growth.

The best source of wisdom is the Bible. That one book contains the wisdom of God, the wisdom of the ages, eternal truths, eternal principles, eternal practices and much more. Bible study is very, very important to personal growth. Reading or listening to the Bible is an important daily habit to grow in wisdom.

There is also the knowledge of the day. There are certain areas of life that the Bible is silent on. We have to look around and search for that. Wisdom (principles) stays the same, but knowledge changes every generation. We are people of the times as well as people of eternity.

Scripture makes a distinction between wisdom and knowledge. Proverbs 8:10-11 says, *"Receive my instruction, and not silver, and knowledge rather than choice gold. For wisdom is better than rubies, and all the things one may desire cannot be compared with her."*

For example, when it comes to setting up an office, managing people, or managing money, you can find principles in Scripture, but in order to find best practices, sometimes you must search for those.

This Year's Calendar

Let us talk about this year's calendar and your next 365 days. Late December is a great time to work on your personal growth plan. However, it is better to start planning now if you have not already done so, regardless of the time of year it is.

Most of us grossly overestimate what we can accomplish over the next few weeks and we grossly underestimate what we can accomplish over the next year. The key thing is to determine to act. Determine the start date and end date for your personal growth calendar.

Four Ways to Approach Your Calendar

1. Abandon Annually

Start by taking a look at the year. Abandon annually refers to getting away from your normal environment, circumstances, and work to rest, meet new people, and see things from a vastly different perspective.

One of the most important things to plan is your vacations. When are you going to abandon everyday life? Plan to go on at least one pure vacation in which you do not work. Look at taking different types of vacations (e.g., long weekends, one to two week blocks of time, etc.). Place those strategically on your calendar. If finances are an issue, be creative in finding good opportunities.

Next add at least one or two big conferences to your calendar. Here, I am referring to several day events, not just half day or all day. These in-person conferences are great opportunities to learn and connect. But before you go to these conferences, determine what outcomes you are looking for and write those down. That intentionality makes big a difference—deciding beforehand what you want to see happen makes it more likely good things will happen.

2. Measure Monthly

Plan to have 12 checkpoints on your calendar where you measure how you did over the previous 30 days. This does not have to be the same day of every month.

There needs to be a monthly time for review by you. Run the tapes of what has happened over the previous 30 days. What did you do right? What did you do wrong? What could you have done better? As Steve and Tara Connell teach, **"There is no failure; only feedback."**

Before a month starts, ask yourself: "Who am I going to be mentored by?" Perhaps once a month meet with a coaching network to review your growth plans over the previous 30 days. Have a point of mentoring from someone who is ahead of you. Do not let a month go by where you are not sitting under the mentoring of someone for at least three to six hours. Since you are the average of the five people you spend the most time with, you need to be around some minds that are better than yours.

In summary, you need a Mentoring Day and an Evaluation Day. Experience is not the best teacher. **Evaluated experience is the best teacher.**

3. Withdraw Weekly

Have you ever wondered why calendars have a weekly cycle (i.e., seven days in a week)? Have you ever wondered why God created the world in six days and rested on the seventh? God modeled and established the Sabbath as a holy day, as a day of rest, renewal, and refreshment because He knew we needed that.

*"Remember the Sabbath day, to keep it holy. Six days you shall labor and do all your work, but the seventh day is the Sabbath of the LORD your God. In it you shall do no work: you, nor your son, nor your daughter, nor your male servant, nor your female servant, nor your cattle, nor your stranger who is within your gates. For in six days the LORD made the heavens and the earth, the sea, and all that is in them, and rested the seventh day. Therefore **the LORD blessed the Sabbath day** and hallowed it."(Exodus 20:8)*

The Sabbath is a good day to evaluate your spiritual and personal life. It is a good day to review your previous week and plan your upcoming week. The Sabbath is a good day to review your journal entries from the previous week. It is a good day to read, listen, and watch things that help you grow. Be sure to have a journal with you to write down thoughts as they come to you.

Each week, plan to read books to help you grow in knowledge. You are preparing for something here. Never leave home without a book. That way when you have to wait, you can be doing something constructive.

What should your read? Read some books on theology, some on philosophy, and some on best practices written by experts on how to do specific things very well. In these books is found the knowledge of the day, not necessarily the wisdom of the ages.

4. Divert Daily

As much as possible, plan your day in advance. **It is a good habit to review your plans for the next day before going to bed at night** so your subconscious mind can solve problems and come up with inspired ideas while you are sleeping.

There are certain things you need to plan in your calendar every single day. One of those is your meeting with God (i.e., your sacred time). A good discipline is "No Bible, no breakfast!" Other good investments of your time include exercise and quality time with your spouse and children. Ideally work this out ahead of time.

In summary, four ways to look at your calendar include Abandon Annually, Measure Monthly, Withdraw Weekly, and Divert Daily.

Prayer Power

Heavenly Father, thank You for the precious gift of life. I dedicate this upcoming year to You. Lead me to be a good steward with my time, talent, treasure, and temple and to maximize all that You give me over this upcoming year. Help me to learn, grow, and be a better person a year from now, more like You and closer to You. In Jesus' name, I pray. Amen and hallelujah!

Study Guide

Questions:

Q: Which passage from the Gospel explains the principle that "A good idea rarely sneaks up on you. You have to go looking for it."
A: *"Ask and it will be given to you; seek, and you will find; knock and it will be opened to you."* (Matthew 7:7).

Q: What are the four ways to look at your calendar?
A: Abandon Annually, Measure Monthly, Withdraw Weekly, and Divert Daily.

Q: How frequently do you need to measure your progress?
A: Measure Monthly. Plan to have 12 checkpoints on your calendar where you measure how you did over the previous 30 days.

Simple Action Step:

Ask God how much time (an hour? a day?) He wants you spend in coming up with your one year growth plan. Then put that time slot down on your calendar and commit to making it happen.

CHAPTER 8

SETTING SMARTT GOALS

Turning Goals into Actionable Items

"You are never too old to set another goal or dream another dream!"
—C.S. Lewis

For much of my adult life, I set written goals to have something to aim for and help steer my choices. That definitely made a big difference in my life. However, it was not until I began my leadership coach training that I really understood what SMARTT goals are and the importance of them.

As mentioned in the first chapter, I launched my very first *I Was Busy, Now I'm Not*™ coaching program in May 2011. Steve and Tara Connell, two participants from New Zealand, soon became very good friends even though this was the first time we ever met.

Recognizing that Steve and Tara are master communicators and extraordinary coaches, I invited them to teach the lesson in my coaching program about "Setting SMARTT Goals." Much of the teaching in this chapter comes from what they shared.

It was during this teaching about SMARTT goals that Tara shared the anonymous poem titled "*The Value of Time.*" That was the first time I had ever heard that poem and it really resonated favorably with my spirit. The poem concludes with, "The clock is running. **Make the most of today!**"

How do we make the most of today? Setting goals to work toward is important. Goals provide us with a framework within which we can make decisions about what we will do and not do.

James 2:20 says, *"... faith without works is dead."* Setting goals is the first step of the "works" part of that scripture. We always have the opportunity to set goals because as C.S. Lewis says "You are never too old to set another goal or to dream another dream."

That particular mantra was the guiding stone for a Christian man whose funeral Steve and Tara attended the week before their teaching about SMARTT goals. That man's name was John. Steve said he mentioned John during his presentation because every now and again someone crosses your path who reminds you time is indeed precious, so choose to make the most of it.

Steve was introduced to John by a friend at church two weeks before his death at age 85. The first time he met Steve, John glared into Steve's eyes and asked him to apply to be a director of a Christian organization he was involved with. John then invited Steve to his place for a chat. Steve was stunned with that, but went to see John to learn a little more about him.

John was a very successful business man. He was Dutch and did very well at making money. John had a tremendous heart for the poor and for those who could not look out for themselves. So for the last 25 years of his life, he devoted himself to funding missions and businesses in Romania, Indonesia, Uganda, and India, and being active in political areas there that affect families. John set up several charitable organizations, including a big youth camp.

John was always ready to give advice. Steve thought, "I want to spend time with you. You are an important person for me. John stewards his money well." Then John died quite suddenly and Steve and Tara found themselves at his funeral wondering what all this meant.

There were about 500 people at John's memorial service. When his life was analyzed and spoken about by many, many people, John impressed Steve and Tara as a guy who was on purpose for the Lord—a true servant of God. John was on fire for the Lord and on the go. At the time of his death, there were probably 50 or 60 people in that room who had something they were doing with this 85 year old man at that time.

This reminded Steve of how precious time was. When Steve visited John at his home a few weeks earlier, he asked, "**What is the secret of jamming so much in your life?**" John replied, "Dear boy, **very precise goals and very clear deadlines.**"

SMARTT Goals

"A goal is not a goal unless it is SMARTT."

As you see in the spelling above, there are two T's at the end of SMARTT. That is not by accident. Many coaching organizations refer to "SMART" goals, standing for Specific, Measurable, Attainable, Relevant, and Time-Framed. Steve added a second "T" for Trackable. Having been an accountant in the past, Steve likes to be able to track progress.

- Specific: defined, clear, precise
- Measurable: observable, quantitative measures to evaluate achievement—find a way to measure the goal
- Attainable: causes you to stretch out and grow within your capabilities—depends only on you
- Relevant: care enough about goal to make it a priority, relevant to the role or context you are currently planning for
- Time-framed: has a start and finish date; realistic and achievable
- Trackable: set short-term objectives/signposts along the way; monitor progress via pre-set markers

The "S" in SMARTT stands for Specific. This is about making sure you define exactly what you mean, very clearly and very precisely. You need to describe in detail what you mean and make sure that you do not have anything foggy, general, or vague.

For example, if you set a goal to "write a book," that is very vague and non-specific. What kind of a book do you intend to write? Who is it going to be reaching? It is more effective to say, "I want to write a book that inspires and empowers young and old in the church community to dream." That would be a more specific definition of the book that you want to write.

After you have the Specific part of your goal established, the next step is to have a Measurable aspect. Your goal needs to be observable and you need to be able to measure it in some way. You must have a quantitative or numerical measure that actually allows you to evaluate your achievement progress.

The question to ask is "How will you or others know that you have achieved your progress?" In response to that you might say, "I am going to write a book and have it published by December 2014." Or you might say, "I am going to write a book that has 12 chapters and 150 pages." Either way, this is adding a measurable quality to your book writing goal.

The "A" in SMARTT is about being Attainable. The thing about attainable is it actually has to be something that is within your capability. But it also has to be something that causes you to stretch and grow.

Extensive research shows that people who are high achievers like to set moderately difficult goals that are nevertheless still attainable. It is in the stretching and reaching that something special happens to you and your growth as a person. So your attainable goal needs to cause you to stretch out and grow and to reach for new dimensions.

Being attainable also means it is something that depends only on you. You do not want to find yourself relying upon other people to do something in order for you to reach your goal.

The example that we can use with the book is, "I want to sell 100,000 copies of my book." Now that certainly would be a stretch for most people, but it would mean that you are dependent on other people buying the book and you cannot control other people's choices. So what you can say instead is, "I will introduce the book to 12 different marketing and distribution networks by the end of December 2014." That is likely a stretch for you, but it is also within your capabilities and depends only on you.

The "R" in SMARTT stands for Relevant and is really about carrying enough about your goal to make it a priority. Your goal needs to be relevant to the season that you are in, to the role that you are playing, and to the context that you are currently planning for. For example, if you are writing a book, your role might be author or it might be product development or marketing for your business.

Here are some good questions to ask when determining if a goal is relevant for you:

- On a scale of 1 to 10, how important is this goal to me?
- If I did not achieve this goal, how would I feel?
- What things am I prepared to put aside to make this goal happen?

As I was writing this *I Was Busy, Now I'm Not*™ book and thought about answering these questions about relevance, I realized writing the book is 10 out of 10 for me. I would be terribly disappointed if I did not write the book because God has given me important keys to being a good steward with time that are working in my life and I know those can help many other people. Failing to achieve my goal of writing this book would actually fail to carry out an important desire in my heart that God put there.

The first "T" in SMARTT stands for Time-Framed or Time-Sensitive. "Framed" means you have a start date and finish date, framing your goal. Your dates need to be realistic and achievable. Depending on the length of the book, saying "I am going to write a book and have it finished next week" would be completely unrealistic and unachievable for most people. However, there are a few people who could realistically achieve this goal with enough motivation.

Continuing with the example of writing your book, instead of saying "I am going to write a book within a year," you are more likely to achieve this goal if you say, "Starting on June 1st, I will begin writing a book and have that ready to go to the printer by December 15th." Now you have a start date and a finish date.

The second "T" in SMARTT stands for Trackable. This is very helpful because it gives you a chance to monitor your progress and put up little sign posts along the way so you can see how you are tracking in terms of achieving success. If for some reason you are falling short or some unexpected things come up, you can revise your mini time table so that you can still meet your end time frame.

The other benefit of this is that having little wins along the way helps you stay a lot more motivated to keep going and pressing on to set higher goals. Again using the example of writing a 12 chapter book by December 15th, let us break that down. You might say, "I am going to write one chapter every two weeks, writing 500 words per day, five days per week. Then you have little sign posts, little objectives, to meet along the way.

Most people tend to be aware of SMARTT goals at some level, but often they are unaware of what really gives them horsepower and what really lifts them off the page to become reality. They also are not aware of what things can block the outworking of the goals.

What Gives SMARTT Goals Horsepower?

"People often complain about the lack of time, when the lack of direction is the real problem."

—**Zig Ziglar**

What Steve Connell noticed over years working in businesses and as a coach for small to medium businesses, is that many people established SMARTT goals, but lacked traction and did not get there when he went to assist them to implement these goals.

As Steve analyzed the problems and situations more closely, he noticed the goals they set lacked direction because the direction they chose to go was not consistent with God's plans and purposes for their lives.

Jeremiah 29:11 reads, *"For I know the plans I have for you, plans to prosper you, not to harm you, plans to give you hope and a future."*

Before meeting Jesus, Steve looked at this scripture mostly from a New Age perspective. Now as a follower of Jesus, Steve routinely asks his clients, "Is what we are doing here in accordance with God's plan for you?"

If it is not clear or he cannot get a precise answer to that, Steve encourages his client to pray first and then seek the counsel of many, including mentors and elders. If it is a big decision, Steve recommends getting some prophetic insight because that helps you know you are on purpose.

Heading the right direction gives horsepower to follow through with your goals. The second thing that gives your SMARTT goals horsepower is clarity.

Clarity is painting a very clear, compelling mental picture of what you desire. The thing about working through the SMARTT goals process is that to be able to answer each of the steps of S-M-A-R-T-T, you are actually starting the journey towards fulfilling the goal because you are creating a mental picture for yourself as you are describing what it is specifically that you are working towards.

The more clearly you can describe what you are moving toward and the more detail you can paint into the picture of your goal, the more you are breathing life into what it is that you want to achieve.

As you create a clear and compelling mental picture, what you are doing is directionalizing your thought life and providing a strong focal point for heaven to move as you plan to breathe life into each aspect of your SMARTT goal.

In the Bible, the first example of setting clear SMARTT goals appears in Genesis 1. As God spoke into being what He already pictured, He was very systematic, precise, and time-specific about what He created. God is a God of order and planning—always. That is His very nature.

Finally, the most important thing that gives SMARTT goals true and everlasting power is inspiration, revelation, and illumination from Holy Spirit. He is the power Source. I call this "the God factor." One day of favor from God can be worth more than a lifetime of labor.

Before ascending into heaven 40 days after His resurrection, Jesus told his disciples, *"But you shall receive power when the Holy Spirit has come upon you."* *(Acts 1:8a)*

In summary, what gives SMARTT goals horsepower are direction, clarity, and inspiration, revelation, and illumination from Holy Spirit.

Key Blockages—Beware!

There are a few blockages that you need to be aware of when thinking about achieving your SMARTT goals.

The first one is competing demands on your time. People who set goals tend to be very focused and determined. And sometimes they put unrealistic demands on their time frames.

You might have a number of things that you are trying to do at once and those competing demands actually make your timelines unrealistic. So ask yourself, "Have I set things out for myself that are going to then cause me to have a sense of pressure because of competing demands?"

The impact of your goal and your timelines on other people can also get in the way as well.

A second obstacle to achieving your goals is trying to achieve too many goals at one time. Three to five goals is the recommended maximum for high achievers to focus on. However, in my opinion, this is too many goals to aim for at once.

As I coach more and more leaders about leveraging time, I am coming to understand the tremendous power of laser focus and doing ONE thing really well. I think you are likely to have much greater impact in a year if you focus on completing one major goal or project every quarter, than if you try to do several significant things at once. This is the power of less.

According to Tim Ferris, author of *The Four Hour Work Week*, "The only way you will form long-lasting habits is by applying the power of less—focus on one habit at a time, one month at a time, so that you will be able to focus all your energy on creating that one habit."

The strategy for success in *The Greatest Salesman in the World* is similar, namely to focus on one goal or one habit for 30 days before moving on to the next one.

Trying to achieve too much too fast can create problems, especially with work-life balance. This causes problems with relationships, which are the currency of the Kingdom of God and business.

When a coach begins chatting with someone in business about what they want to achieve, that owner or executive may say they want to double or triple their turnover in a certain time frame. But after looking closely at the implications of that decision on the leader's family, a good coach will draw his/her attention to the impact of that decision.

A good coach will not allow business owners and executives to make decisions that have long-term negative consequences on their health and family. Instead that coach will negotiate at the onset with the business owner or executive, advising him to go slower on his goals and reduce the workload so there is time to invest with the family. And once the owner or executive focuses on that, he/she can get a balanced view of what is going on in his/her life.

It is really critical to look at who else is impacted by the decision or the goal that you are making or setting right now. **If you are married, include your spouse in all important decisions.** According to Jack Serra, "The businessman's ministry in the marketplace will only advance to the extent his marriage permits."

A third blockage to achieving your SMARTT goal is unclear motivation. When you think about your goal, you need to be very clear about what that goal will get you.

Let us take a look again at our example of writing a book. If I ask, "What will the goal of writing your book get you?", you might respond:

- It will establish credibility and position me as an expert in that area.
- It will allow me to reach a broader audience.
- It will allow me to send my messages internationally.
- It provides a useful tool for executive coaching.
- It will open the door for me to speak, get paid well for sharing my message, and spread the message further.
- It will help fulfill a longstanding dream and desire of my heart.

These reasons provide a compelling motivation when the going gets tough to keep you on track toward achieving your goal. That provides the context to think about while moving toward your goal.

In summary, three big obstacles that can get in the way of you achieving your SMARTT goal include:

- Competing demands on your time. To address this, ask "Will these demands make my timelines unrealistic?"
- Trying to achieve too many goals all at once. The ideal solution is to focus on only ONE thing (goal) at a time.
- Unclear motivation. To resolve this, keep asking "What will that goal get me?"

4 WHAT Model

Before setting SMARTT goals, Steve and Tara Connell recommend leading clients first through the "4 WHAT Model."

Here is how that works. The coach asks the client, "In your role of _____, what is your goal?" For example:

- In your role of parent, what is your goal?
- In your role of business owner, what is your goal?
- In your role of product development, what is your goal?
- In your role of marketing, what is your goal?

This sets up the 4 WHAT questions:

1. WHAT is your goal?
2. WHAT does that mean specifically?

3. WHAT will that get you?
4. WHAT steps will you take to get there?

After the client answers the 4 WHAT questions to their satisfaction and the coach's satisfaction, then they are ready to complete the SMARTT goals process using those answers.

Let me give a personal and real example. If a coach asked me today "What is your goal?", I would say "to have *I Was Busy, Not I'm Not*™ be a New York Times best seller by December 2014."

A good coach would then ask me, "What does that mean specifically?"

With time to reflect, my answer would be: "I plan to submit my completed, edited, proofread copy of my book to Morgan James Publishing by May 20, 2014. David Hancock, the founder, told me his company can have my book published and available for purchase in print and via electronic media within three months. Therefore, I expect that process will be completed by August 20, 2014. I will contact David and Carl Townsend to ask to schedule a live meeting with both of them and me in May to discuss best ways to mass market my book. Since David is recognized by NASDAQ as one of the world's most prestigious business leaders and is reported to be the future of publishing and Carl has 80 million contacts, I know this connection will be explosive. These are simple and strategic things I know I can do that by doing them everything else will either be easier or unnecessary. These actions will bear enormous fruit."

My coach might then ask, "What will that get you?"

My reply would be: "This will brand me globally as *The Time Doctor*™, recognized world-wide as the pre-eminent thought leader with stewarding and leveraging time, both in the Christian and non-Christian marketplace. My book will be used by millions of people around the world as a study guide for life groups. My gift will attract leaders of integrity and great wealth who have a vision to change the world for good and God. Leaders from all over the world will seek me out to take quantum leaps in their businesses and ministries. Our team at Empower 2000 will assemble and facilitate hundreds and thousands of high performance dream teams (Master's Mind Marketing™ tribes) that communicate weekly with groups of business and thought leaders around the world. Ultimately this will empower dreams of millions of people, bringing God's love, hope, power, and salvation to several billion people."

Obviously this is quite inspirational and compelling for me, making achieving this goal a must. So, I will do whatever it takes to make this goal a reality.

Summary

Let us summarize the most important principles of setting and achieving SMARTT goals.

- Always be on purpose in the Lord's plan for you. This keeps the fire going.
- Look at the 4 WHAT Model.
- Develop precise, SMARTT goals.
- Deal with the potential blockages.
- Monitor, Monitor, Monitor!
- Review, Review, Review!
- Reset when necessary.
- Celebrate along the way. It has to be fun.

Prayer Power

Father, I praise You as the Master with the master plan. I confess that I have wasted much of my life because I have had wishes instead of SMARTT goals. I acknowledge that a successful life is a productive life and those who have clear written goals are much more productive. I ask for Your guidance in setting my SMARTT goals. Help me to overcome struggles I have in this area of my life and bless with me with an accountability partner or coach to help keep me on track. In Jesus' name I pray. Amen and hallelujah!

Study Guide

Q: What does SMARTT stand for?
A: Specific, Measurable, Attainable, Relevant, Time-Framed, and Trackable

Q: What gives SMARTT goals horsepower?
A: SMARTT goals get horsepower with direction, clarity, and inspiration, revelation, and illumination from Holy Spirit.

Q: What are common blockages to achieving your SMARTT goals?
A:
1. Competing demands on your time
2. Trying to achieve too many goals all at once
3. Unclear motivation

Q: What are the 4 WHAT questions?
A:
1. What is your goal?
2. What does that mean specifically?
3. What will that get you?
4. What steps will you take to get there?

Simple Action Step:

During your sacred time in your sacred place ask, "Father, what is ONE thing I can do in the next three months that by doing it everything else will either be easier or unnecessary?" Write down your answer. Then turn that ONE thing into a SMARTT goal and find someone to coach you. I think you will be amazed at what happens.

CHAPTER 9

UNCOMMON JOURNALING FOR DIVINE DESTINY

Experiencing God in Extraordinary Ways for Extraordinary Fruit

"Journaling is the key to unlock your dreams!"

—**Joseph Peck**, M.D.

Journaling is a great spiritual habit—in fact the best spiritual habit I have ever had in my life. Journaling is the lead domino of my life. It will absolutely change your life when you embrace it. Jesus wants you to learn to hear His voice to experience the adventure of your lifetime!

In John 10:27, Jesus says, *"**My sheep hear My voice**, and I know them, and they follow Me."*

I used to think that journaling was not for me. While I kept detailed written records for lots of things and had written goals, it was not until I was introduced to the FCA (Fellowship of Christian Athletes) Bible in the fall of 2001 that I first got interested in journaling.

I first began journaling daily on January 1, 2002, and have rarely missed a day ever since. Nowadays, I often invest several hours journaling daily and hence my branding as *The Journal Guy.*

Why invest time with a habit like journaling when I can be doing so many other things that are fun or that can lead to success? The answer lies in the extraordinary benefits and fruitfulness I have seen in my own life.

Whenever I use the word "uncommon," I mean inspired by Holy Spirit for a God-sized result. I have learned how to journal to experience God in extraordinary ways for extraordinary fruit and now I want to teach you.

Why Journal?

Why make journaling a daily habit? Unless you are convinced that journaling is going to make a big difference in your life, you are likely to give up on this great habit before it is firmly established. But when your why is big enough, the how will work itself out.

Pastor Rick Warren, author of *The Purpose Driven Life*, says the purpose of the Bible is to change lives and the purpose of preaching is to change lives. The purpose of journaling is to change your life. It is that simple.

There are lots of great reasons to journal. Here are some of my favorites. Journaling:

1. Helps you slow down to meditate on the Word of God. This allows you to hear God's quiet still voice.
2. Allows God to be your Master Coach
3. Builds your faith by helping you remember what God has done
4. Keeps your priorities in order
5. Is a great spiritual habit (discipline)
6. Leads to rest, reflection, and revelation—the tricord of leverage
7. Builds your prayer life
8. Helps you learn and apply valuable life lessons
9. Improves relationships and communication
10. Helps you dream big dreams
11. Helps you get organized
12. Helps you keep your commitments

Most people live unexamined lives. They repeat the same errors day after day and fail to learn much from their choices and mistakes. Most people do not know why they exist or where they are going. Journaling will help you examine your life.

Jim Rohn, known as "America's Foremost Business Philosopher," wrote "If you're serious about becoming a wealthy, powerful, sophisticated, healthy, influential, cultured and unique individual, keep a journal. Don't trust your memory. When you listen to something valuable, write it down. When you come across something important, write it down." Rohn said keeping a journal is one of three treasures to leave behind for the next generation. The other two are your photos and your library.

When done properly, journaling helps you experience God in extraordinary ways. This is not theory to me. It is reality. And I have coached hundreds of other people to journal daily to experience God too. I am a friend of God. What about you?

Slowing Down to Get in Synch With God

In Psalm 46, God promises He will be exalted among the nations if we will just be still and know that He is God. God will be exalted in your home, neighborhood, church, business, and ministry when you are still and know I AM. He is sufficient. You see, it is the presence of God that changes you and your circumstances. Everywhere God is miracles happen.

Be still and know that I AM God.
I will be exalted among the nations.
I will be exalted in the earth!
(Psalm 46:10)

In Psalm 1, my favorite Psalm in the Bible, God promises we will be blessed when we delight and meditate on His Word morning and night. Obviously, meditation implies more than just thinking about something. It also involves a change in behavior (i.e., action).

Blessed is the man who walks not in the counsel of the ungodly, nor stands in the path of sinners, nor sits in the seat of the scornful; But his delight is in the law of the LORD, and in His law he meditates day and night. He shall be like a tree planted by the rivers of water that brings forth its fruit in its season, whose leaf also shall not wither; and whatever he does shall prosper. (Psalm 1:1-3)

We live in a hurry-sick culture! But to be spiritually healthy, you must ruthlessly eliminate hurry from your life. That is because love and hurry are incompatible. When Jesus was asked what the Greatest Commandment is, He said love God and love people.

Love in any relationship is spelled T.I.M.E. To have an authentic walk with Jesus, time is required. Something good may have to give way in order to give God your first fruits—the first and best of your time. Some practical tool must be employed to slow down your RPMs from 10,000 to 5,000 to 500, where you can be at peace with God and be in a condition to hear what the Lord is saying.

One of the best ways to slow down your RPMs is journaling. Here I am referring to keeping a spiritual journal. This involves writing down things you are thankful for, what you hear from God, and other inspired thoughts.

My Five-Step Method for Journaling

I follow a simple five-step method when I journal. The first three steps are the most important. If you only have time for one step, do the first one. Having and maintaining a grateful heart will open more doors for you than you ever dreamed possible.

Step #1: Thank God

By reviewing things from the previous day each morning and giving thanks to God for all things, you are often able to see the hidden treasures in your relationships and circumstances.

It is the glory of God to conceal a matter, but the glory of kings is to search out a matter. (Proverbs 25:2)

Rejoice always, pray without ceasing, and in everything give thanks; for this is the will of God in Christ Jesus for you. (1 Thessalonians 5:16-18)

In his book *Ordering Your Private World*, Gordon McDonald suggests buying a simple spiral notebook for your journal. He recommends planning to write in this notebook every day, but restricting yourself to one page. Every day when you open to the next blank sheet of paper, write the same first word, "Yesterday..." Follow this with a paragraph or two recounting yesterday's events. According to McDonald, this exercise causes a tremendous step forward in spiritual development.

I do this slightly differently and my approach leads to a conversation with God. **When I begin journaling, I start by writing "Good morning Jesus! Thank you for ..."** Then I write down at least seven things I am grateful for. Often the first thing I write down is "Thank You for another good night's sleep in a warm comfortable bed next to my wife." I never take rest or sleep for granted, nor my comfortable bed, nor my wife. When I thank God with a pure heart for something in my life, He usually multiplies it. Consequently, almost every night I sleep like a baby and wake up well rested and in a good mood. And that is a gift.

I continue writing down things I am thankful for, most of them from the day before, but sometimes for meetings and opportunities that day. As I do this exercise, I often remember small things that I would have missed had I not done this. In my experience, some of God's biggest blessings are hidden in the simple and ordinary things of life. Remember, it is the glory of God to conceal things and your glory to find them. (Proverbs 25:2)

There is a protocol for entering the presence of the King and that begins with thanksgiving. We thank God for what He gives to us and we praise Him for who He is.

Enter into His gates with thanksgiving, and into His courts with praise. Be thankful to Him, and bless His name. (Psalm 100:4)

The whole process of renewing your mind and atonement can be summed up in one word, gratitude.

First, you believe that there is a good God who owns everything and has a master plan, which includes you. Second you believe that God gives you everything you need to fulfill the desires of your heart because He placed those within you. And third, you relate yourself to Father God by a feeling of deep and profound gratitude.

Many people who order their lives rightly in all other ways are kept in poverty by their lack of gratitude. Having received one gift from God, they cut the connection with Him by failing to make acknowledgment.

The more gratefully we fix our minds on God when good things come to us, the more good things we will receive, and the more rapidly they will come. This happens because the mental attitude of gratitude draws the mind into closer touch with the Source from which the blessings come.

Draw near to God and He will draw near to you. (James 4:8a)

Gratitude brings your whole mind into closer harmony with the creative energies of the universe. Gratitude alone can keep you looking toward God and prevent you from falling into the error of thinking of the supply as limited. To do the latter is fatal to your hopes. There is a Law of Gratitude, and it is absolutely necessary that you should observe the law to get the results you seek.

In contrast, the moment you permit your mind to dwell with dissatisfaction upon things as they are, you begin to lose ground. To permit your mind to dwell upon the inferior is to become inferior and to surround yourself with inferior things.

On the other hand, to fix your attention on the best is to surround yourself with the best, and to become the best.

Step #2: Listen to God and write down what you hear

After giving thanks to God for what He has given me and let me partake of, I invite Jesus to dine with me and then write down what I hear.

"Behold, I stand at the door and knock. If anyone hears My voice and opens the door, I will come in to him and dine with him, and he with Me." (Revelations 3:20)

I often write, "Jesus, I am ready to listen to You. Speak Lord, I love to listen to Your voice." or "Jesus, I am all ears. I invite You to come in to dine with me." I expect Him to meet with me and speak to me. My childlike faith comes from believing Jesus that His sheep hear His voice and follow Him. I am a sheep. What about you?

"My sheep hear My voice, and I know them, and they follow Me." (John 10:27)

According to Dr. Mark Virkler, founder of Communion With God Ministries, **the four keys to hearing God's voice are Stillness, Vision, Spontaneity, and Journaling**. Dr. Virkler teaches "Hearing God's voice is as simple as quieting your mind, fixing your eyes on Jesus, tuning to spontaneity, and writing."

While the idea of having a conversation with God may be new to you, it is not new to God. God walked and talked with Adam and Eve in the Garden of Eden. And Jesus came to restore our relationship with God, not just to save us.

Good relationships are always two-way. Both parties listen and speak (or write). If your idea of praying to God is telling Him your requests or writing them out, then you are missing out on the most important aspect of the relationship, namely listening to Him. A monologue is not sufficient in a healthy relationship with God.

Imagine you are a loving father or mother walking down a path with one of your children. You talk some and so does your child. If your child asks you a question, you will answer them right away if you know the answer. You want to bless your child. If your child frequently thanks you for whatever you give him or do for him, you will want to continue to shower him with blessings.

Pastor Adrian Rogers, one of my favorite preachers, used to have a frequent short message on American Family Radio that I loved. He would say, "**Why don't people obey God?** It is because they don't know Him. Knowledge of God leads to trust in God. Trust in God leads to obedience to God. And obedience to God leads to blessings by God." The best way to know God is by reading or listening to His Word, the Bible.

In her book *LORD, Teach Me to Study the Bible in 28 Days*, Kay Arthur writes, "I am convinced God's message through the prophet Hosea is the same as His message to us today: It is absolutely essential for each of us—man or woman, young or old—to understand the importance and value of knowing the truth. In other words, you must know the Word of God, the Bible."

*Hear the word of the LORD, You children of Israel, for the LORD brings a charge against the inhabitants of the land: "There is no truth or mercy or **knowledge of God** in the land. By swearing and lying, killing and stealing and committing adultery, they break all restraint, with bloodshed upon bloodshed. Therefore the land will mourn; And everyone who dwells there will waste away with the beasts of the field and the birds of the air; Even the fish of the sea will be taken away. **My people are destroyed for lack of knowledge.** Because you have rejected knowledge, I also will reject you from being priest for Me; Because you have forgotten the law of your God, I also will forget your children. (Hosea 4:1-3,6)*

Step #3: Record your REST

I place tremendous value on getting adequate rest because I know that is extremely important to steward my time and life well and to live my big dreams.

Consequently, I log my rest in my journal nearly every morning as one of the first things I do. I write down when I went to bed, what I did before going to bed, how fast I fell asleep, how well I slept, when I got up, and any dreams I can remember.

I rarely set an alarm clock anymore, but rather go to bed early enough so I can wake up early and feel well rested. I call Maui (my dog) "my God alarm clock" because she usually wakes me up early in the morning to be fed. Her timing is usually impeccable, just when I am thinking about getting up. After feeding Maui and letting her outside briefly, I usually go back to bed and lay still resting and reflecting in a semi-alpha state (partial dream state) with godly thoughts flowing through my mind before getting up 30-60 minutes later. I frequently say quietly, "Speak Lord, I love to listen to Your voice," expecting Him to speak to me. This is a special time and place for me where I hear God most clearly and where He reveals uncommon ideas and strategies to me. I am never short on creative ideas.

When I get up, I am anxious to start journaling as soon as possible to record the thoughts the Lord has given me before they slip out of my conscious mind. I cherish what God reveals to me.

I never take rest or sleep for granted, nor my comfortable bed, nor my wife. When I thank God with a pure heart for something in my life, He usually multiplies it. Consequently, almost every night I sleep like a baby and wake up well rested and in a good mood. And that is a gift. Rest is a place where creative ideas and solutions are birthed. And it is ideas that change the world.

Michael Stay, a good friend and outstanding strategic planner, taught me the tricord of leverage is rest, reflection, and revelation. I never forgot that. I understand now that rest leads to reflection and reflection leads to revelation and illumination as well as character transformation. God is much more interested in who we become than what we do for Him.

What you do first thing in the morning sets the tone for the rest of your day. If you think you are not a morning person, my counsel to you is, "Get over it. God is a morning God."

I believe insufficient time for rest and reflection often leads to poor planning, poor choices, and suboptimal results. In addition, fatigue leads to less patience and compromised relationships.

I cannot overemphasize the importance of rest to optimize your use of time. You are most creative when you are well rested and relaxed. That is where flow happens in your mind and spirit. The most important lesson I have ever learned in my life is this, "To be spiritually healthy, you must ruthlessly eliminate hurry from your life!"

Jesus says, *"**Come to Me, all you who labor and are heavy laden, and I will give you rest.** Take My yoke upon you and learn from Me, for I am gentle and lowly in heart, and you will find rest for your souls. For My yoke is easy and My burden is light."* (Matthew 11:28)

The question is, "Will you slow down and come to Jesus for His rest?"

Step #4: ABIDE

The first fruits of your time is exactly that—the first and best of your time. That is why I usually go to my sacred place for my sacred time as the very first thing in my day. Because my most important meeting of the day is my meeting with God, before I do anything else, I want to thank God and hear what He has to say. That is how I come out of the gate charging and motivated to win the race for that day.

When I get to my sacred place, I usually kneel down and pray for a few minutes before starting to journal. Most mornings I journal before reading or listening to the Bible because I want to capture thoughts I heard while lying in bed before they slip out of my mind. Under the heading "ABIDE" in my journal, I record what I did during my meeting with God and the order I did it. This includes anything I read or prayed, specific Bible passages, specific prayers, and specific chapters in books. This helps me discern how the Lord is leading me, so I can stay on the right path.

Your word is a lamp to my feet and a light to my path. (Psalm 119:105)

In his book *Secrets of the Vine*, Dr. Bruce Wilkinson shared these three simple commitments he made to the Lord that revolutionized his life and led to tremendous fruitfulness in his ministry:

- Get up at 5 a.m. each day to read my Bible;
- Write a full page in a daily spiritual journal;
- Learn to pray and seek Him (God) until he found Him.

Step #5: Inspired Thoughts

I keep a bulleted list of thoughts and ideas that came to my mind while I was lying in bed resting and reflecting and that I receive while abiding in my sacred place. By writing these down early, they most accurately represent what I heard. Writing these down frees my mind from having to think about them anymore. Also, I am more likely to act on them, even if that is a week, a month, or a year later.

My Sample Journal Entry (using the five-step method)

January 4, 2014 (Saturday)

(Step #1) Good morning Jesus. I look forward to this sacred time with You more than anything else. Thank You for…

- Another good night's sleep in a warm, comfortable bed next to Julia. I don't take that for granted, including my sleep and rest.
- The Sabbath day and my understanding of the importance of keeping that holy.
- My long nap yesterday evening with the opportunity to listen carefully to Your holy Word.
- Your instruction yesterday to "Come out of Babylon!"
- Prompting me to call Rick Saunders and our extraordinary conversation.
- My ability to hear Your voice and my desire to obey You and follow You.
- Branding "Lord and Saunders" with LORD and the huge breakthroughs that Rick and Joey are having.
- Helping me through another week financially.
- The warning that "2014 is a make it or break it year!"
- The three blog posts I created yesterday with two at empower2000.com and one at yourdailyblessing.com.
- The wonderful vegetable lasagna dinner I had with Julia and for our good conversation. Thank You for Julia clearly expressing her concerns.

(Step #2) *Joseph, you are most welcome. I like how you are starting your mornings expressing your thanks and writing down your inspired thoughts. The joy you have and express is contagious. Your connection to Rick and Joey Saunders is very significant. Trust Me with your finances. Do not try to push open doors when there is resistance. Rick can help you close deals and communicate your value. You must express/communicate your need for help to have others step in to help you. If I take care of the birds of the air, I certainly will take care of you. Enjoy your day! Know that you are richly blessed and highly favored.*

Lord, what is ONE Thing I can do today that by doing it everything else will be easier or unnecessary?

DECLUTTER your desk.

(Step #3) REST: I went to bed at 10:30 pm exhausted after a long hard work day, a two hour nap, eating dinner, and then reading the Bible for 90-120 minutes. I fell asleep quickly and slept like a baby until 4:35 am when Maui got me up. After feeding Maui and letting her outside briefly, I went back to bed. I lay still resting and reflecting in a semi-alpha state with godly thoughts flowing through my mind before getting up at 5:40 am.

(Step #4) ABIDE: When I got up, I immediately went to my sacred place for my sacred time. I knelt down and prayed for a few minutes before starting to journal. I read *The Power of a Praying Husband* Chapter 12 (Her Fears), *The Power of a Praying Parent* Chapter 3 (Securing Protection From Harm), and my Ultimate Vision.

(Step #5) Inspired thoughts

- The primary benefit of journaling is FOCUS.
- "Come out of Babylon!"
- Call Rick Saunders on Sunday morning. Record his audio testimony for IWBNIN, journaling, and my coaching. Create a short video from that. Post that at moretime777.com. Then email IWBNIN prospects regarding three remaining spots.
- Call Lyman Eddy regarding his payment.
- Schedule meeting with David Sluka regarding focus and book coaching program.
- Email David Hancock regarding IWBNIN and Carl. Schedule a meeting. "I need your help."
- Invite Ken McArthur to IWBNIN.
- Call John Burpee regarding Denise Lograno.
- Make your own 20-30 minute video regarding the Sabbath. Script the message and record that to make it concise and to the point.

- Schedule webinars with Rick Grubbs, Lisa Jimenez, and Vic Johnson.
- 2014 Goal: Plan to launch Master's Dream Academy.
- Set clear goals for 2014.
- Order *More Than A Carpenter* to give to your father as a birthday present.
- Give Rick Saunders *You²* book

The Best Time to Journal

After observing my own behaviors and those close to me, I feel confident saying you are most likely to succeed in establishing journaling as a firm habit when you journal early in your morning.

If you are like me and most other people, your days often spiral out-of-control as they go along, seeming to get more and more hectic. New and unexpected things pop up to distract you. I know I am definitely most productive in the first few hours of the morning. When I save an activity for the evening, it is easy for that to get bumped out of my schedule by other pressing matters.

What you do first thing in the morning sets the tone for the rest of your day. Even though you may think you are not a morning person, God is a morning God."

Before Joshua led two million people into the promised land, God commanded, *"This Book of the Law shall not depart from your mouth, but you shall meditate in it day and night, that you may observe to do according to all that is written in it. For then you will make your way prosperous, and then you will have good success."* *(Joshua 1:8)*

The very first Psalm of the 150 Psalms declares, *"Blessed is the man whose ... delight is in the law of the LORD, and in His law he meditates day and night. He shall be like a tree planted by the rivers of water that brings forth its fruit in its season, whose leaf also shall not wither; and whatever he does shall prosper."* *(Psalm 1:1-3)*

One of the reasons Daniel could interpret dreams and was promoted to second in command for the most powerful kingdom in the world was that he had the habit of praying to God and thanking him three times a day for years. Daniel 6:10 says, *"Now when Daniel knew that the writing was signed, he went home. And in his upper room, with his windows open toward Jerusalem, he knelt down on his knees three times that day, and prayed and gave thanks before his God, as was his custom since early days."*

God tells us to give him our first fruits, not our leftovers. When you start your day poorly or sluggishly, what kind of results do you expect? If you fail to receive your guidance or instructions from the Lord during abiding time early in the day, who are you really living that day for?

In his book *Secrets of the Vine*, Dr. Bruce Wilkinson writes, "Set apart the kind of time that will build relationship. Some Christians I know try to have their meaningful personal times with God just before bed, but I have yet to find a respected spiritual leader throughout history who had devotions at night. **Unless you get up early, you are unlikely to break through to a deeper relationship with God.** Set aside a significant time and a private place where you can read and write comfortably, think, study, talk to God out loud, and weep if you need to. In abiding, what happens on the surface does not count; what is happening inside does."

My recommendation is to start each day by going to your "secret place," kneeling down, and praying for a few minutes. My personal habit is to say the "LORD's Prayer" several times along with a few other short prayers. Then I read the Bible or listen to it using iTunes. I nearly always start journaling within the first 30 minutes.

Blessings to journal early in the morning to set the tone for fruitful days!

Recommended Time to Invest Journaling

If you have not been journaling at all or you journal very little (e.g., once a week or less), my recommendation is to start journaling 15 minutes per day.

Building your habit of journaling can be compared to training to run your first marathon. If you have not been running at all, it is usually a poor idea to go out and run 15 miles on your very first day. There are exceptions of course such as Ryan Hall, the top qualifier for the U.S. Olympic marathon team for the 2008 Beijing Olympics. One day when Ryan was 15 years old, he told his father he wanted to run a full lap (15 miles) around Big Bear Lake.

Live surveys of audiences during my introductory journaling webinars have shown that about half of the people attending journal regularly. Of those people who journal regularly, about half journal 15-30 minutes per day on average and half journal for 30-60 minutes per day. No one I surveyed journaled for more than 60 minutes per day on average. I journal hours daily, but that is because God prepared and equipped me to teach others. Mark Jarvis taught me that a leader must jump six feet if he wants his followers to jump six inches.

Just as someone who sets a goal of running a marathon must start off gradually with his training, you must start off gradually with this new habit of journaling. Usually, when you add something new to your daily schedule, something else must come out. So decide beforehand what you are going to give up as you add the new habit of journaling.

I like what Rick Warren says, "The best way to begin is to begin!" So, my recommendation to you is to choose a journaling method that most appeals to you and start with that. As the Nike slogan says, "Just do it!"

Start journaling as soon as possible. Do not wait until you finish reading this book. Getting started is as easy as 1-2-3. See the "Getting Started Journaling" section below.

Journaling Online (for Power)

> *Remember His marvelous works which He has done, His wonders, and the judgments of His mouth, (1 Chronicles 16:12)*

Journaling online is journaling on steroids. By "online," I mean using a computer, tablet, or Smart phone. You do not necessarily have to have an internet connection.

The first two years I journaled, I did so writing by hand in a notebook. I used *My Utmost for His Highest* journal with 365 daily devotionals by Oswald Chambers. Typically I began each morning reading the Bible first and then journaling using the PRESS method (Pray, Read, Examine, Summarize, and Share). I absolutely loved this habit and found myself ushered into the presence of God on a consistent basis.

Then in the Fall of 2003 while listening to an eleven CD set by Rick Warren titled "Preaching For Life Change," I heard Rick mention in a very short segment (about 20 seconds) that he does his "quiet time" online. That sounded radical to me. I thought, "With so many potential distractions on the computer, how could online journaling and 'quiet time' be compatible?"

However, because I had tremendous respect for Rick Warren and his book *The Purpose Driven Life*, I reluctantly made an agreement with God to do a 30 day trial of online (computer) journaling starting on January 1, 2004. That date was very significant because I had already made a commitment to God to bump up my average daily quiet time from two to four hours. That is another miracle story that I will not discuss here.

My deal with God was that I would continue online journaling after the one month trial period only if I saw significant fruit within 30 days. Otherwise I was going back to what I knew and loved—journaling by hand. Within days of journaling on my computer, I saw the benefit and the rest is history. As someone with extensive experience journaling by hand and on the computer, I estimate journaling on the computer is at least 10 times more effective than journaling by hand.

During the past several years, I have encouraged and trained many people to journal online. In that process, I have seen numerous people who have journaled extensively for years by hand using notebooks, make the switch to journal on their computers. Every person I talked to who used to journal by hand and then took the plunge to journal on the computer experienced new insights and breakthroughs—everyone.

Here are eight great reasons to journal online:

1. Meditate in a deeper, richer way on the Word of God
2. Rearrange: Cut and paste contents from one place to another
3. Plan: Become more organized. Set goals and achieve them.
4. Review: Much easier to go back, read, and review
5. Observe: Keep track of important emails and communications (analogous to letters in old days)
6. Remember: Greatly facilitates remembering what the Lord has done
7. Action: Follow through better with your commitments
8. Share your God stories with the world via the world-wide web

I am in the process of seeking partnerships to develop and mass market life-changing apps for tablets and Smart phones to make online journaling easy, affordable, and readily available to millions of people around the world. If that is something you can help me with, please contact me. I believe these apps will create a revolution with many more people being able to recognize the voice of their heavenly Father.

Getting Started Journaling

But be doers of the word, and not hearers only... (James 1:22)

Getting started journaling and being successful is as easy as 1-2-3. Here are the three steps:

Step #1: Make a commitment.

Complete the "Journaling Accountability Form" below or at www.journal777. com/accountability

Whether you are just starting the habit of journaling, changing your method, starting to journal online, or trying some new journaling software, it is essential to have clear written goals to achieve maximum results and impact. Remember, a goal is not a goal unless it is SMARTT (i.e., Specific, Measurable, Attainable, Relevant, Time-Framed, and Trackable).

Since it typically takes three to five weeks to firmly establish a new habit like this, I recommend making a commitment to journal every day for five weeks (35 days). And remember to follow the KISS principle—Keep It Simple Students. Start with a simple journaling method and pace yourself (i.e., plan to grow gradually).

Step #2: Find someone who will hold you accountable to achieve the goals you set. Accountability is the password to your future!

Step #3: Start journaling within 24 hours. There is no time like the present.

Journaling Accountability Form

Turn your journaling habit into a SMARTT goal

Starting ___/___/___ (date), I commit to journal every day for the next 35 days.

How long are you going to journal each day (minimum)?

- 5 minutes
- 15 minutes
- 30 minutes
- Other (specify)

When are you going to journal?

- Within 30 minutes of getting up
- Within one hour of getting up
- Within one hour before going to bed
- At another set time (Please specify _____)

Where are you going to journal? Where is your secret place?

- In a notebook or blank journal by hand (Specify where)
- On my desktop or laptop computer at home or work (Specify where)
- On my tablet or Smart phone (Specify where)
- Other (Specify where and on what)

What method are you going to use to journal? (See UJFB book)

- Yesterday... Prayer Power (recommended)
- PRESS (Pray, Read, Examine, Summarize, Share)
- ACTS (Adoration, Confession, Thanksgiving, Supplication)
- Other (Please specify)

What tool are you going to use for your journaling?

- Notebook (away from computer)
- Word processor (on computer or tablet)
- Blog (on computer)
- Other (Please specify)

Who is going to hold you accountable with this habit and how often?

What are your top three goals from journaling?

- _____
- _____
- _____

Your Printed Name: _____
Your Signature: _____
Date: _____

Conclusion

Your most important meeting of the day is your meeting with God. God not only wants more of your time; He also wants your first fruits—the best of your time. Journaling is a great way to record your journey with God. **Your most important journal entries are your conversations with God.**

Many people pray on the run rather than scheduling regular time for prayer. They miss out on the most important relationship, namely their relationship with God. Praying on the run is like building a marriage on the run—it does not work.

Choose to invest quality time listening to God to follow Him and abide in Him more deeply. Your moments in God's presence are the most important ones. You cannot become an authentic Christian on a diet of constant activity, even if the activity is all church related. The archenemy of spiritual authenticity is busyness. It is time to be still, reflect, and listen. Choose life!

"See, I have set before you today life and good, death and evil, in that I command you today to love the LORD your God, to walk in His ways, and to keep His commandments, His statutes, and His judgments, that you may live and multiply; and the LORD your God will bless you in the land which you go to possess. But if your heart turns away so that you do not hear, and are drawn away, and worship other gods and serve them, I announce to you today that you shall surely perish; you shall not prolong your days in the land which you cross over the Jordan to go in and possess. I call heaven and earth as witnesses today against you, that I have set before you life and death, blessing and cursing; therefore choose life, that both you and your descendants may live." (Deuteronomy 30:15-19)

Blessings to journal daily for long enough to encounter God in a deep way!

Prayer Power

Heavenly Father, I praise You as the greatest Journaler ever. Thank You for leaving the Bible as Your love letter to me. Thank You for Your disciples who wrote down what You told them to leave a legacy. Change my heart and inspire me to develop a daily consistent habit of journaling that helps me grow closer to You to become all You intended me to be. Thank You Jesus! Amen and hallelujah!

Study Guide

Question:

Q: What is the purpose of spiritual journaling?
A: The purpose of spiritual journaling is to change your life by connecting with God. It is that simple.

Q: How does journaling help us to learn from our mistakes?
A: Typically, we repeat the same errors day after day. We do not learn much from our choices and mistakes unless we take time to think about them. We do not know why we exist or where we are going. Journaling helps us examine our lives.

Q: How can you make journaling a daily habit?
A: Complete the Journaling Accountability Form above.

Simple Action Step:

Tomorrow, begin your journaling with "Good morning Jesus! Thank You for..." Then make a list of things you are grateful for.

CHAPTER 10

CONQUER FEAR

Stop Defeating Yourself and End Self-Sabotage

"The only person keeping you from achieving your goals is you."
—Lisa Jimenez

In early 2013, I joined *The Champions Club*, which turned out to be one of my best business investments ever. Vic Johnson founded and leads that. He is a personal development expert and the founder of asamanthinketh.net.

In the last quarter of 2013, Vic led those participating in The Champions Club through a 12-week course called Maximum Momentum. The purpose was to focus on one main goal to create massive momentum to start the New Year well. That certainly happened for me. This book is just some of the fruit of that.

During the Maximum Momentum course, Vic introduced me to a book by Lisa Jimenez titled *Conquer Fear!* After purchasing that book, I read it entirely in a few days because it was so good. This is the best book about conquering fear I have ever read.

While journaling during my sacred time in early 2014, I was prompted to contact Lisa to ask to host her on a webinar titled *Conquer Fear!* When I called Lisa, she immediately agreed. The webinar with Lisa was extraordinary.

Lisa Jimenez is a professional speaker and author who has helped thousands of people shatter their self-limiting beliefs and finally get the breakthrough success they want. She is a thought leader when it comes to personal productivity and creating unstoppable momentum.

Lisa says, "**Fear is the dominant problem in your life today**. When your fear of success, fear of failure, or fear of rejection is exposed, you break through their control over you."

Let me ask you:

- How many opportunities have you missed because fear has stopped you?
- What wall do you need to break through?
- What glass ceiling do you need to shatter?
- Have you ever said to yourself, "If they really knew me, they would not love me?"
- Do you want to stop making the same mistakes over and over again?

If you have wrestled with questions like these, you are not alone. If you want to change your life for the better—spiritually, emotionally, physically, and mentally—then Lisa can help you do just that.

What Keeps You from Living Your Dreams?

The one thing that keeps people from the life they dream of is fear. People live every day in their fear. They are afraid of:

- Losing their wealth
- Losing their loved ones
- Being themselves
- Looking foolish in front of others
- Growing up and being responsible
- Making the wrong decision
- Making a commitment
- Life itself

Truth #1: Fear is the dominant problem in your life today.

To conquer your fear, you must first identify which fear has control over you and your behaviors. Is it the fear of failure, fear of rejection, fear of success, or all three? Your second step is to interrupt the bad habits that you have developed as a means of protection from this fear?

Fear is a part of every person's life. It serves to help us grow and draw us nearer to God. Overcoming fear is a part of every success story.

Truth #2: Fear is a gift that was instilled in you as a means of protection and a way to bring you closer to God.

Some fear is healthy. For example, all people are born with three inborn fears—fear of falling, fear of loud noises, and fear of abandonment. These fears are instilled in you to keep you safe.

There is a distinction between reacting to fear and acting in fear. Most adults do not differentiate between reacting with instinct and acting with their intellect when dealing with fear. Instead they react instinctively to their fear by running from it, ignoring it, sabotaging their efforts, or quitting their pursuit of the very dream they said they wanted so they will not have to face their fear. The solution is to be aware of the gift fear can bring you and to know how to have power over your fear.

Truth #3: When you run from or deny your fear, you leave the gift unopened.

Most people do not receive the gift that comes from facing their fears. Instead they make excuses for what they don't have. They may blame their lack of success on their upbringing, lack of a good education, lack of money, their boss, an unsupportive spouse, the government, or something else.

But anytime you choose to blame others, you make yourself a victim and lose power to overcome your circumstances. **The foundation of liberty is responsibility**.

What do you fear? Is it commitment, rejection, responsibility, growing up, confrontation, not measuring up, loss, change, or something else?

All of these surface fears keep you from exposing the core fear, the true cause of the anxiety, depression, and destructive behavior that choke your dreams to death. These symptoms of fear can be conquered by exposing the core fear that hides behind them and breaking through the negative beliefs they represent.

Lisa Jimenez believes out of all the fears we say we have, we are controlled by only two core fears, namely the fear of failure and the fear of success.

Conquer Your Fear of Failure

"The difference between greatness and mediocrity is often how an individual views a mistake."

—Nelson Boswell

Fear of failure can paralyze you. You may never dream big because you do not want to take a risk. You may abandon your goal in mid-stream so you will not have to face the consequences of possibly failing at it.

When you change your view of failure, your fear of it will change. In reality, failure is just one more step toward your dreams. The secret of success is to never quit. When you fall down, get back up.

To have victory over the fear of failure, embrace these truths:

- Failures are the steps you take that bring you to success.
- Failure helps you to depend on others more.
- Failure can help bring you closer to God.
- Failure is a small part of the big picture.
- If you have not had a failure in the last year, you are not growing enough.
- Growing hurts. But not growing destroys.
- Failure is a teacher to show you what not to do.
- Failure is a great way to help you say "I am sorry" more.
- Failure is a way to show you that you cannot do it alone.
- **Failure is a sign that you need to stop, assess, and change.**
- Failure is a part of life.
- Failure was never intended to kill you or to stop you.

When you understand that failure is part of your journey to success, then you can withstand the temptation to quit when you encounter adverse circumstances that last a long time.

My brethren, count it all joy when you fall into various trials, knowing that the testing of your faith produces patience. But let patience have its perfect work, that you may be perfect and complete, lacking nothing. (James 1:2)

It is important for you to reject rejection. Most people do not want rejection. However, those people who understand the law of averages embrace rejection because they know the money is in the no's.

Let us assume that it takes 10 phone calls or conversations to get a "yes" to an offer you are making. Let us further assume that you earn $200 each time a person accepts your offer. Then on average you make $20 per phone call or conversation. When you view it this way, all of a sudden making the calls seems worthwhile.

Your lack of courage is costing you—a lot. Lack of courage affects your relationships, your sales, your level of success, and your ability to live an authentic life.

In summary, hear are ways to conquer your fear of failure:

- Change your view of failure and your fear of it will change
- Reject rejection
- Regain your courage
- Cultivate your childlike thinking
- Practice extravagant thinking
- Dream extravagantly
- Take a courageous account

Conquer Your Fear of Success

Most people secretly and often unknowingly attribute a lot of pain to being successful. Their beliefs about success are terrifying. The real problem is they do not even realize they have this fear. Being aware of a problem is the first step to overcoming it.

Nelson Mandela said, "Our deepest fear is not that we are inadequate. Our deepest fear is that we are powerful beyond measure. It is our light, not our darkness, that most frightens us. We ask ourselves, who am I to be brilliant, gorgeous, talented, and fabulous."

Is it fear of letting your light shine brightly that is keeping you from taking risks and pursuing your dreams?

One of the first steps to conquering your fear of success is to cultivate your faith. Make a commitment to invest quality time with God each morning. I say "morning" because how you start your days sets the tone for what happens in your day. When you decide that your meeting with God is your most important meeting of the day, then you are open to receiving your marching orders from Him every day.

To have victory over the fear of success, embrace these truths:

- Success means living the life you love.
- Success is knowing who you are in God's plan.
- Success is not always measured by financial gain.
- Becoming financially secure is really about your faith in God and depending on Him to supply your needs.
- Becoming wealthy may be a part of your success.
- Money gives you choices.
- Successful people have balance in their lives.
- 98 percent of the millionaires in the United States have been successfully married for over 20 years.
- Successful people know how to play as well as work.
- Success means to dream as well as to act, to believe as well as to plan.
- Money is not your God.
- The LOVE of money is the root of evil.
- **You can have control over your time when you are successful**.
- It is possible to enjoy life and still become wealthy.
- Success is obeying the unique plan God has for you.
- It is possible to be a great parent and become successful.
- If you are in a relationship with the living, loving God, you are already successful.

In summary, three steps to your breakthrough include exposing your true fear, revealing any negative beliefs, and adopting a powerful belief system.

Here are seven truths Lisa teaches to conquer your fears and live your big dreams:

Truth #1: Fear is the dominant problem in your life today.

Truth #2: Fear is a gift that was instilled in you as a means of protection and a way to bring you closer to God.

Truth #3: When you run from or deny your fear, you leave the gift unopened.

Truth #4: When your fear of success or fear of failure is exposed, you breakthrough their control over you.

Truth #5: Your belief system is the driving force behind your behaviors and your results.

Truth #6: Your everyday habits are broadcasting your belief system, your fear, and your unmet needs loud and clear.

Truth #7: Change your beliefs and you change your behavior. Change your behaviors and you change your results. Change your results and you change your life.

For more information about these and other topics relating to fear, I recommend you read Lisa Jimenez's book *Conquer Fear!* and visit her website at www.rx-success.com.

Prayer Power

Heavenly Father, thank You for this teaching about conquering fear. I confess that there are many times I have not obeyed You or taken action in my life because of fear of something. I acknowledge that fear is a symptom of a deeper issue. Teach me to become aware of my fears when they first start to surface and help me recognize the underlying lies or beliefs that are not true. May Your holy Word be my truth and buckler (Psalm 91:4). In Jesus' name I pray. Amen and hallelujah!

Study Guide

Questions:

Q: According to Lisa Jimenez, what are the two core fears that control us?
A: Fear of failure and fear of success.

Q: The fear of failure is pretty easy to understand, but why do so many people fear success?
A: Most people secretly and often unknowingly attribute a lot of pain to being successful. Their beliefs about success are terrifying. The real problem is they do not even realize they have this fear.

Simple Action Step:

Pray and ask the Lord to show you what your biggest fear is. Then ask Him to lead you through overcoming it.

CHAPTER 11

THE 60-60 EXPERIMENT

Staying Connected to God

"When you stay connected with God, fruit happens!"
—**John Burke**, Soul Revolution

We see a lot of people who boast about their accomplishments. I used to be like that before God humbled me big-time. In my early 40's, I had $1.6 million in my retirement account. Less than 10 years later, my retirement account was empty and I was $200,000 in debt.

There even came a day when I had to call up a friend in desperation asking this person to sow a financial seed in my life so I could pay my electric bill to keep the lights on in my home and pay my internet bill so I could stay in business.

For someone who had managed his money well for most of his life and always paid his credit card bills in full when due, this was a big change and in the wrong direction.

Fortunately, by God's grace and mercy I was restored. Within five months of starting the 60-60 Experiment, my $200,000 debt was wiped away.

What happened to result in this amazing turnaround?

I let go and let God!

I finally gave up trying to do things my way. Oh, I had been meeting with God almost every day—reading or listening to the Bible, praying frequently, and recording my journey with Him in my journal. Everyone who knows me well would say without a doubt that I love Jesus.

But **what I was missing was knowing how to surrender to Holy Spirit moment-by-moment** and how to make fine tune adjustments in how I navigated through my days.

Big breakthroughs started happening in my life when I began The 60-60 Experiment in October 2011. For example, within just a few days of starting:

1. I completely cleared my Inbox for Gmail, something I had wanted to do for several years, but never could before no matter how hard I tried. And realize I am a very organized person. The best I could ever do before was get down to maybe 30 or 40 emails.
2. I resumed my weekly email with prayer requests to about 40 intercessors. This was something I had done for 6-12 months before letting this good habit slip away. I had wanted to resume this for more than a year, but for some reason I could not until starting the 60-60 Experiment.
3. I was prompted to ask for recommendations for LinkedIn and received eight encouraging ones within 24 hours. In the prior three years, I only had one recommendation because I never made this a priority. Without the encouragement from those inspiring recommendations, this book never would have happened.
4. I began video messaging, something I had wanted to do and known how to do for one to two years, but somehow just could not get started.

What is the 60-60 Experiment?

The 60-60 Experiment is a plan to intentionally connect with God every 60 minutes for 60 days. The purpose is to develop a radically-responsive relationship with God.

The 60-60 Experiment is a simple habit to receive divine guidance moment by moment by allowing Holy Spirit to be the Navigator for your life.

Years ago, it used to be that a plane was flown by both a pilot and a navigator. The pilot flew the plane while the navigator gave directions because he knew precisely where the plane was and where it was going. The 60-60 Experiment is about letting Holy Spirit be the navigator for your life, while you serve as the pilot.

The 60-60 Experiment is a global movement initiated by John Burke with his book *Soul Revolution* and the associated website.

> "Through real-life stories, explore how God takes imperfect people, regardless of their past, and leads them into a relational journey toward their heart's greatest desire. Experience how a moment by moment connection to God with wide-open willingness fulfills our deepest longings and transforms us into life-giving people."

How does The 60-60 Experiment work?

For 60 days you intentionally connect with God every 60 minutes. You can remind yourself every hour in a variety of ways. For example, you might have your mobile phone alarm clock sound or vibrate every hour, put sticky note reminders in several places (e.g. on your computer, bathroom mirror, refrigerator, car dashboard, etc.), or put a little string on your finger. Whatever works best for you is fine.

Reorient—Doing Life with God 60-60, [Source: pp 49-51 of *Soul Revolution* by John Burke]

For the first 45 years of his life, Frank Laubach lived a pretty average life. He was an American-born Christian living in a remote part of the Philippines, yet on his 46th birthday he wrote in his journal:

> I no longer sense that life is all before me, as I had a few years ago. Some of it is behind—and a miserable poor part it is, so far below what I had dreamed that I dare not even think of it. Nor dare I think much of the future. This present [moment], if it is full of God, is the only refuge I have from poisonous disappointment and even almost rebellion against God.

Yet that year, 1930, despite the disappointment of life so far, something changed. By 1970, when Laubach passed away, his influence had spread worldwide. The Encyclopedia Britannica notes he was perhaps the single greatest educator of modern times, voted "Man of the Year" in America.

In the last 40 years of his life, Laubach developed the Each One Teach One literacy campaign, used to teach 60 million people to read in their own language, all across the globe. He wrote over 50 books and became an international presence in literacy, religious, and governmental circles—having an influence on poverty, injustice, and illiteracy worldwide. His influence spread to presidents as well as across the underdeveloped areas of the world.

What changed in that year of 1930 for Frank Laubach? Many who have written about him say little about his spiritual life because they do not understand it, but in his own words, 1930 was the year he began to experiment with a reorienting, revolutionary kind of prayer that changed everything.

In Laubach's journal published under the title *Practicing His Presence*, in January 1930 he wrote:

> Two years ago, a profound dissatisfaction led me to begin trying to line up my actions with the will of God about every 15 minutes or every half hour. People said it was impossible. I judge from what I heard that few people are really even trying that. But this year I have started to live all my waking moments in conscious listening to the inner voice, asking without ceasing, **"What, Father, do You desire this minute?"** It is clear that this is exactly what Jesus was doing all day every day.

Laubach began an experiment—much like the 60-60 Experiment—in moment-by-moment continuous conversation with God. Laubach wrote:

> It is exactly that "moment by moment" surrender, responsiveness, obedience, sensitiveness, pliability, "lost in His love," that I desire to explore with all my might.

After 30 days, Laubach already felt a joy he had never experienced in 16 years as a Christian.

> This sense of cooperation with God in little things is what so astonishes me... I need something and turn around to find it waiting for me. I must work, to be sure, but there is God working along with me. God takes care of all the rest. My part is to live this hour in continuous inner conversation with God and in perfect responsiveness to His will, to make this hour gloriously rich. This seems to be all I need think about.

After 60 days, Laubach wrote:

The experiment is interesting, although I'm not very successful thus far. The thought of God slips out of my sight for I suppose two-thirds of every day, yet this thing of keeping in constant touch with God is the most amazing thing I ever ran across. It is working. As I analyze myself I find several things happening to me as a result of these two months. This concentration upon God is strenuous, but everything else has ceased to be so. I think more clearly, I forget less frequently. Things which I did with a strain before, I now do easily and with no effort whatever. I worry about nothing, and lose no sleep. If He is there, the universe is with me. My task is simple and clear.

Nearly a year later, Laubach wrote:

It is difficult to convey to another the joy of having broken into the new sea of realizing God's "hereness." How I wish, wish, wish that a dozen or more persons [would try this] ... and write their experiences so that each would know what the other was finding as a result! The results, I think, would astound the world. At least the results of my own efforts are astounding to me.

Can you hear it in Frank Laubach's journals—this eternal quality of living that comes flowing up from within as we do life in relationship with God?

Testimony about the 60-60 Experiment

From personal experience and coaching others, I know the 60-60 Experiment makes a big difference and often very fast. Here is what one of my coaching clients wrote a few days after starting the 60-60 Experiment:

For me, I set my phone alarm to go off every hour between 7 AM and 7 PM. My first observation is how quickly an hour goes by. If nothing else this was a great exercise in realizing the brevity of "time" and how easily it slips by, whether we spend it wisely or not. Another thing I found out is how easy it is to tune God out at times: "No LORD, I'm too busy doing my own thing right now. No time to talk or listen. Check back with me in an hour." That is ridiculous, right? But unfortunately I found this to be sooo true.

What I did enjoy when I took time to connect with Him was the moment by moment fellowship of actually feeling that He is right there every step of the way, involved in my moment to moment activities, and so readily available either to receive thanks from me or spur me on through the next hour. This exercise has really given me insight in a new way of walking with God and being aware of His presence moment by moment. For the time being, my phone alarm will keep on beeping, reminding me at every hour that Papa is ready and willing both to speak and to hear His daughter's voice. Thank you LORD!

So what about you? Are you willing to try something new for 60 days to see what happens?

Blessings to do the 60-60 Experiment!

P.S. I highly recommend watching this short video about the 60-60 Experiment and Frank Laubach's story: http://empower2000.com/the-60-60-experiment/

Prayer Power

Father God, thank You for this teaching about staying connected to You on a moment by moment basis. I confess that there are many times I drift my own way and forget that You want to be the Navigator for my life. I acknowledge that when I stay connected to You, fruit happens. Help me to apply the 60-60 Experiment in such a way that I get addicted to You and Your presence. In Jesus' name I pray. Amen and hallelujah!

Study Guide

Questions:

Q: What was Dr. Peck missing that when he added resulted in the amazing turnaround in his life?
A: Knowing how to surrender to Holy Spirit moment by moment and how to make fine tune adjustments in how he navigated through his days.

Q: What is the 60-60 Experiment and what is its purpose?
A: The 60-60 Experiment is a plan to intentionally connect with God every 60 minutes for 60 days. The purpose is to develop a radically-responsive relationship with God.

Simple Action Step:

Begin the 60-60 Experiment today and stick with it.

CHAPTER 12

LIVING ON PURPOSE

Living Life as God Intended

"The key to discovering all you are meant to do and be is to wake up to the big dream God has given you and set out on the journey to achieve it!"
—**Bruce Wilkinson**, author of *The Dream Giver*

How do you create an extraordinary life? One important aspect is knowing your purpose and living that daily. The number one time waster by far for most people is not living on purpose. If the ladder of your life is leaning against the wrong wall, you can never reach your intended destination.

God has a plan for your life and it begins with your purpose. *"For I know the thoughts that I think toward you, says the LORD, thoughts of peace and not of evil, to give you a future and a hope." (Jeremiah 29:11)*

Do you know that most Americans dread getting out of bed? They do not enjoy their work and are not happy with their lives because they do not have purpose that gets them excited. But that does not have to be the case for you.

In his classic *A Christmas Carol*, Charles Dickens teaches us how to live through the story of Ebenezer Scrooge. For most of his life, Ebenezer has been mean and miserly, thinking only of himself and gathering money. But in a single night, his heart turns from stone cold to piping hot after a dream he has on Christmas Eve. His dream starts with a visitation by Jacob Marley's ghost, who is wearing a ball and chain and tells Scrooge that he will be visited by three spirits that night.

The first of the spirits, the Ghost of Christmas Past, takes Scrooge to Christmas scenes of his boyhood and youth. This stirs his gentle and tender side by reminding Scrooge of a time when he was kind and innocent.

The second spirit, the Ghost of Christmas Present, takes Scrooge to several different scenes—a joy-filled market where people are buying things for Christmas, a miner's cottage where people are celebrating Christmas, and finally Bob Cratchit's family feast, where Tim is happy despite being seriously ill. The spirit informs Scrooge that Tiny Tim will die soon unless circumstances change.

The third spirit, the Ghost of Christmas Yet to Come, shows Scrooge Christmas Day one year later. Tiny Tim has died because Cratchit could not afford to provide him with proper care. The spirit then shows Scrooge scenes involving the death of a "wretched man," who turns out to be Scrooge. Seeking a different outcome, he pledges to change his ways in the hope of creating a more promising future.

Scrooge awakens on Christmas morning full of love and joy. He spends the day with Fred's family, and anonymously sends a prize turkey to the Cratchit home for Christmas dinner. The following day, he gives Cratchit a raise, and becomes like a father to Tiny Tim. A transformed man, Scrooge now treats people with kindness, generosity, and compassion.

What changed Scrooge's behavior? It was his change in purpose. Scrooge was mean and miserly when his focus was on making money. When his purpose became people, joy followed.

According to Gary Keller in his book *The ONE Thing: The Surprisingly Simple Truth behind Extraordinary Results*, "Dickens shows us a simple formula for creating an extraordinary life: Live with purpose. Live by priority. Live for productivity."

Live by Purpose

Gary Keller says: "Dickens reveals purpose as a combination of where we're going and what's important to us. Our purpose sets our priority and our priority determines the productivity our actions produce."

Here are my favorite points that Gary makes about living on purpose:

- **Who we are and where we want to go determine what we do and what we accomplish**.
- Ask enough people what they want in life and you will hear happiness as the overwhelming response.
- One of the biggest challenges is making sure our life's purpose does not become a beggar's bowl, a bottomless pit of desire continually searching for the next thing that will make us happy.
- Happiness happens on the way to fulfillment.
- Dr. Martin Seligman, past president of the American Psychological Association, believes there are five factors that contribute to our happiness: positive emotion and pleasure, achievement, relationships, engagement, and meaning. Of these, he believes engagement and meaning are the most important.
- Financially wealthy people are those who have enough money coming in without having to work to finance their purpose in life.
- Purpose is the straightest path to power and the ultimate source of personal strength—strength of conviction and strength to persevere. The prescription for extraordinary results is knowing what matters to you and taking daily doses of actions in alignment with it. When you have a definite purpose for your life, clarity comes faster, which leads to more conviction in your direction, which leads to faster decisions. When you make faster decisions, you will often be the one who makes the first decisions and winds up with the best choices. And when you have the best choices, you have the opportunity for the best experiences.
- Purpose also helps you when things do not go your way.
- When you ask yourself, "What's the ONE Thing I can do in my life that would mean the most to me and the world, such that by doing it everything else would be easier or unnecessary?" you are using the power of the ONE Thing to bring purpose to life.

Live by Priority

In Lewis Carroll's classic "Alice's Adventures in Wonderland," Alice asks the Cheshire Cat, "Would you tell me, please, which way I ought to go from here?" The cat replies, "That depends a good deal on where you want to get to." Alice then says, "I don't much care where." In response the cat says, "Then it doesn't matter which way you go."

This reveals the close connection between purpose and priority. In *The ONE Thing*, Gary Keller writes, "Live with purpose and you know where you want to go. Live by priority and you will know what to do to get there."

Gary goes on to explain how "priority" actually comes from a Latin word meaning "first." The word remained singular (i.e., priority, not priorities) until the 1900's when the meaning morphed to "something that matters."

Here are my favorite points that Gary makes to live by priority:

- The truth about success is that our ability to achieve extraordinary results in the future lies in stringing together powerful moments, one after the other. What you do in any given moment determines what you experience in the next.
- The further away a reward is in the future, the smaller the immediate motivation to achieve it.
- "Goal Setting to the Now" will guide your thinking and determine your most important priority.
- Writing down your goals and your most important priority is your final step to living by priority.

Live by Productivity

"Productivity isn't about being a workhorse, keeping busy, or burning the midnight oil. It's more about priorities, planning, and fiercely protecting your time."

—Margarita Tartakovsky

According to Gary Keller, "Productive action transforms lives." Each day we do something. The question is, "Is that something in alignment with the purpose for which you were created and is it moving you toward your top priority?"

Gary says, "The most successful people are the most productive people. Productive people get more done, achieve better results, and earn more in their hours than the rest. They do so because they devote maximum time to being productive on their top priority, their ONE Thing. They time block their ONE Thing and then protect their time blocks with a vengeance."

Most people think there is not enough time to be successful, but Gary believes there is when you block your time. Time blocking is a way of making sure what must be done is done. To do this, block off time in your calendar to accomplish your ONE Thing. **"If disproportionate results come from one activity, you must give that one activity disproportionate time."**

To learn more about Gary's effective method for "time blocking," I recommend reading *The ONE Thing*.

The Power of a Two-Word Purpose Statement

Kevin W. McCarthy is the best-selling author of *The On-Purpose Person: Making Your Life Make Sense.* He is one of the top leaders in the world teaching people how to live on purpose and is branded as "America's Chief Leadership Officer." I first met Kevin in August 2012 on the very first Stewards webinar led by Robert and Cheryl-Ann Needham.

Meeting Kevin was a major turning point in my life. His teaching and coaching made a profound difference in how I live my life as well as my impact. It was Kevin who helped me realize my purpose is INSPIRING LOVE and EMPOWERING DREAMS. Ever since then, that has been my focus. This understanding has shifted everything I do.

When Kevin first released *The On-Purpose Person* in 2009, he "souled" 32,539 copies in just five days. His book became rated as the #1 best-seller for Amazon.com in eight different categories and #5 for all book titles. Since then, Kevin has sold hundreds of thousands of copies of his book.

At www.2wordpurpose.com, Kevin has an outstanding free video teaching about "*The POWER of Your Two-Word Purpose Statement*." In that, he clarifies why so many people are stressed, overwhelmed, and confused so much of the time.

In his survey of a large number of people in his target audience, Kevin reported:

> 63% of respondents said they did not have a written personal purpose, vision, or mission statement. Only 13% of respondents indicated their written purpose statement was guiding their lives daily.

Respondents said benefits of living on purpose include:

- Flushing out what is most important
- Keeping focused and clear
- Making choices more effectively and confidently
- Discerning what is right and wrong for me
- Keeping on track in a crazy world
- Cutting through the haze of confusion
- Helping to love life

Respondents said costs of living off-purpose include:

- Taking on people, activities, and projects I should not
- Wasting time and energy due to lack of focus
- Feeling overwhelmed, depressed, and sad
- My life is run by urgencies and crisis = chaos
- Cannot experience the fullness of life
- I do not have my own voice; I get run over
- No true guidelines or boundaries
- Rudderless and I feel I have no future
- Squandering my talents
- Directionless, discontented, and hopeless
- No map, no meaning, spinning my wheels
- Dreading growing old
- Fear takes me over
- I look back with regret and forward afraid
- Others do not get what I have to give

The "off-purpose" dollar cost was estimated to be more than one million dollars by 46% of respondents.

Obviously, the cost to society with people living off-purpose is huge in many different ways.

Kevin went on to explain why a two-word purpose statement is so valuable. Two words are easy to remember and thus actionable. Two words reflect the DNA of our spirit. Two words keep your purpose simple, making it easy to discern if you are on-purpose or off-purpose. Two words close our devilish loopholes in which we justify our time-wasting behaviors and actions.

To discover your two-word purpose statement:, realize it:

- Answers the question, "Why do I exist?"
- Is singular
- Is a heart matter
- Addresses the past, present, and future
- Integrates all aspects of life
- By definition, it is good
- Is written in a two-word format

Kevin recommends that the first word in a two-word purpose statement be a verb ending in "ing" because that reflects the past, present, and future. For example, my personal purpose statement, "I exist to serve by INSPIRING LOVE," signifies that I was inspiring love, I am inspiring love, and I will be inspiring love.

Kevin says you have only one personal purpose and one work purpose. He recommends starting your personal purpose statement with "I exist to serve by (insert your two-word purpose)." Kevin recommends starting your work purpose statement with "We exist to serve by (insert your two-word purpose)."

These simple statements reflect the fact that you were created for a purpose and that you are on planet earth to serve, not to be served.

Examples of personal two-word purpose statements, include "I exist to serve by …"

- Empowering Expectation
- Liberating Greatness
- Awakening Worth
- Inspiring Hope
- Realizing Abundance
- Rousing Faith
- Embracing Joy
- Igniting Grace
- Revealing Truth

Just as flipping a light switch to "on" turns on the electric power, so living on purpose turns on the spiritual power in your life to accomplish great things with God and through Him. P.O.W.E.R. is an acronym for Precision, Oneness, Written, Energy, and Relationships.

"Precision" in a two-word purpose statement occurs when it is detailed, accurate, specific, in context, defining, identifying, and well-designed.

"Oneness" in a two-word purpose statement means it is holistic (wholeness), authentic, held together, integrated, and strong.

"Written" means your two-word purpose statement is documented, creative and creating, defined yet deeply diverse, directing and regulating, and measurable.

"Energy" in a two-word purpose statement comes from being connected, inspiring, sustainable, and spirited.

"Relationships" in a two-word purpose statement must reflect super-personal (self with higher power), intrapersonal (self with self), and interpersonal (self with others). For example, with my two-word purpose of "Inspiring Love," it is important for me to frequently ask, "How am I inspiring love in my relationship with God? How am I inspiring love in myself? How am I inspiring love in others?"

To better understand what is being shared here, watch Kevin McCarthy's outstanding video at www.2wordpurpose.com. Please be aware that when you come to this web page, it takes about seven minutes before the video starts to play automatically. There is no way to manually advance to the start of the video.

On-Purpose Peace

The following in an excerpt of what Kevin W. McCarthy teaches in *On-Purpose Peace*, an interactive small group guide for Christians reading *The On-Purpose Person*. This powerful, thought-provoking program grips you from the start and equips you to wrestle with God to better understand who He is and who you are within His design, purpose, and plan for your life.

> As Christians we are eternal beings, so time is practically meaningless. Time on earth is finite. As God's children, we are called to be stewards of our time, talent, and treasure. "Time management" is a noble Godly endeavor, but time is irrelevant to eternity.
>
> So if time is meaningless to eternal life, then what is most precious to us? "Our relationships on earth as it is in heaven" are most precious. This

begins with our personal relationship with Christ and extends to our relationship with ourselves. Next, is our covenant relationship with our spouse, then our children and immediate family, including our church family. Last, but not least are our social, work, and play relationships.

The Great Commandment speaks clearly about loving God, ourselves, and our neighbors. Love is the basis of all relationships. Learning to love God, ourselves, and our neighbors transforms and transcends time for our lifetime and beyond. Love, unlike time, is infinite and so, like the Prodigal Son, we tend to squander it in worldly pursuits.

Purpose plays a vital role in the mystery of our faith. Sacraments, such as Baptism, Marriage, and Communion, are defined as "outward and visible signs of an inner grace." Your purpose is similar to a sacrament in that it is an outward expression of the inner grace and mystery of one's relationship with Christ.

Purpose is our identity in Christ and our personal connection to the source of love. Like a light switch being either on or off, we are either connected to Christ or we are not. Christ's love is either in and flowing through us or not there. Thanks to free will, we control the light switch. What we did not control was the fact that the light switch was installed on us by God the Creator.

Purpose is the basis for integrating the relationships and activities of life. When time, rather than purpose, becomes the focal point, we are apt to be so closely looking at the trees that we miss the forest. What could be better than to be with people you love doing what you love to do?

If we are just managing time on earth, then we are truly in the dark spiritually. This places us at a severe disadvantage in our worldly endeavors because we are cut off from the Source and floundering out of our calling. When lost, we strive to be and become, but the effort and, even the success, feel empty and unfulfilling.

Time management has its place in the lives of every Christian. It helps us to better invest ourselves where God has given us stewardship and dominion within his Kingdom.

To be on-purpose begins with a decision to be identified with Christ. Better understanding of who He is helps us to better understand who we are as creations made in God's image. **Being on-purpose is a lifestyle and means being Christ-like more of the time.** The more we bring expression to who Christ is in us, then the more we are in God's will and in cooperation with the God who can redeem our days.

On-Purpose Peace is unlike any Bible study or program you have ever done because it intimately builds and deepens your personal relationship with Jesus Christ so you too can "take heart" regardless of the conditions around you. Experience it for yourself and discover how God has been conspiring for your benefit all along so you can be yourself, prosper, and contribute in ways that only God knows. Your part is to regularly integrate His will into your ways. Experience oneness with God!

"These things I have spoken to you, that in Me you may have peace. In the world you will have tribulation; but be of good cheer, I have overcome the world." (John 16:33)

To learn more, visit www.onpurposepeace.com.

Living Your Big Dreams

In his book *The Purpose Driven Life*, Rick Warren writes, "Being successful and fulfilling your life's purpose are not at all the same issue. You could reach all your personal goals, become a raving success by the world's standard, and still miss the purposes for which God created you... To discover your purpose in life you must turn to God's Word... You were created by God and for God—and until you understand that, life will never make sense.... Nothing matters more than knowing God's purposes for your life, and nothing can compensate for not knowing them."

My life can be divided into two very distinct parts—B.C. ("Before Christ"; before my spiritual rebirth in 2001) and A.D. ("After Death" to myself and my choice to follow Jesus daily). Before committing my life to Jesus, I was living my life primarily for myself with an 80 year perspective. Now I am living my life for God's purposes with an eternal perspective.

After coaching hundreds or thousands of leaders over the past eight years, I have discovered **five things to accelerate your big dreams**: mindset, clarity and focus, SMARTT goals, a coach, and a dream team.

1. Mindset

"For as he (a man) thinks in his heart, so is he." (Proverbs 23:7)
What you think about is extremely important. Ralph Waldo Emerson is quoted as saying, "Sow a thought and you reap an action; sow an act and you reap a habit; sow a habit and you reap a character; sow a character and you reap a destiny." Your thoughts determine the words you speak, the actions you take, the habits you establish, and ultimately your destiny. Since it is your beliefs that drive your thoughts, it is crucial to renew your mind with truth to live on purpose.

Let me share a true story about a major breakthrough I experienced as a result of changes in my thinking. Remember, when you change your thinking, you change your life!

In January of 2013, I signed up for The Champions Club led by Vic Johnson, the founder of asamanthinketh.net. In August 2013, I began participating in weekly webinars led by Vic. On September 30, Vic began a 12-week coaching program called Maximum Momentum. As a result of Vic's teaching and the dramatic changes in my thinking and focus, I began accomplishing more in a day than I used to in a week and more in a month than I used to in a year. This book and the momentum I have with my *I Was Busy, Now I'm Not*™ coaching program are fruit of my changed thinking.

2. Clarity and Focus

The second thing to accelerate your big dreams is clarity and focus. To get where you want to be, you have to know where you are going and the directions to get there. This is so important.

As a dream coach, I see so many people who do not know what they want or where they want to go, and so of course they struggle in their lives. The greater the clarity you have, the greater the favor you will experience.

Reading the book *The ONE Thing* and learning to ask the Focusing Question had a profound impact on me and those I coach. As a result, I am more focused than ever before in my life. And that is leading to tremendous results.

3. SMARTT Goals

The third thing to accelerate your big dreams is SMARTT Goals. It has been said, a goal is not a goal unless it is SMARTT. SMARTT stands for Specific, Measurable, Attainable, Relevant, Time-Framed, and Trackable.

Here is an example of how this works. If someone tells me they want to lose weight, it is clear to me that is not a SMARTT goal. And I can be quite sure that person is unlikely to lose weight.

Now, here are some questions I might ask to turn that person's vague goal into a SMARTT goal.

- How much weight do you plan to lose?
- When do you plan to lose that weight?
- What are you going to do to lose weight?
- How often are you going to exercise?
- What kind of exercise are you going to do?
- How long are you going to do that each time?
- What are your plans to build up to that?
- What changes do you plan to make with your diet?

These sample principles apply to your big dreams. Big dreams are manifested by setting big goals. Big goals are achieved by setting a series of smaller goals.

4. Coach

The fourth thing you need to accelerate your big dreams is a coach. A coach is someone who asks good questions instead of just telling you what to do. A coach provides SEA = Support, Encouragement, and Accountability. Accountability is the password to your future. A coach helps you navigate from where you are to where you want to be. Coaching provides a trusted relationship to grow and be transparent.

Since becoming a coach, I have discovered that **asking is much more powerful than telling**. Getting somebody to think things through for themselves produces more change and gets much better results than giving them advice or telling them what to do. Now, instead of telling or giving advice, I tend to ask questions because I know that when people have light bulb moments, that has a more lasting effect.

I call my coaching Master's Mind Coaching™ (MMC) because it is about seeking the mind and heart of the Master together. When coaching a new client, I tell him (or her) that I come into the coaching relationship as a "zero" even though I have extensive training and experience as a leadership coach, breakthrough life coach, and dream coach. That is because if I come in as a nine or an eight, Holy Spirit can only be a one or a two. But humbling myself and being willing to be coached by Holy Spirit along with my client, allows God to be the Master Coach, leading to bigger breakthroughs and quicker results. This is powerful and creates an environment of holy expectation.

5. Dream Team

The fifth thing you need to accelerate your big dreams is a dream team. Big dreams are always bigger than you and your organization. That is why I believe every big dream needs a dream team.

In 1908, Andrew Carnegie commissioned Napolean Hill to study 500 of the most successful people in the world. After 25 years of research, Hill wrote a 1,100 page book describing 16 common success principles. The very first principle he discussed was mastermind groups. So almost all or all of the most successful people in the world had mastermind groups (dream teams). According to Hill, "The mastermind is the synergy created when people work together towards goals in a spirit of harmony!"

In 2009 I asked the question, "What if we invited Holy Spirit to join a mastermind group?" That is how the idea for Master's Mind Marketing™ (MMM) tribes was birthed. A MMM tribe is a high performance dream team that intentionally seeks the mind and heart of the Master together.

When Holy Spirit is invited, expected, welcomed, and given control rather than man taking control, a super-charged atmosphere is created during the calls and sessions. And it is in this environment that divine ideas, strategies, connections, etc. are revealed.

The goal of the Master's Mind Marketing™ tribes is to come together to collaborate and explore the best and brightest ideas that lead to major breakthroughs and increases in influence and impact.

One of the most common problems with leaders and organizations, no matter how successful they are, is "**Lone Ranger Syndrome**." This usually is the result of focusing on growing their organizations and impact rather than being part of a much bigger dream. Symptoms may include feelings of being isolated, stuck, or not living up to their potential. **To achieve your big dreams, you must partner with others to achieve their big dreams**.

A second challenge many leaders face is communication. They do not understand how to draw in the nets, how to capitalize on relationships they have built with people over their lifetimes. They do not have the strategies and systems to communicate regularly and effectively with people in their networks and to build a global community.

A third common challenge is clarity. When leaders are not clear on their purposes and dreams, they often lack focus and find themselves doing too many things, thereby losing effectiveness. Without the help of a dream expert, few leaders are able to see how their dreams intertwine with those of others and if they do, how to bring the people and dreams together in a forum that benefits everyone.

The missing link for great success for most entrepreneurs and organizations is the dream team and a master maestro to facilitate that.

During the past several years, I have had the privilege of assembling and facilitating numerous dream teams (Master's Mind Marketing™ tribes) with leaders around the world. And we have seen some absolutely amazing things happen as a result.

At Empower 2000, we are masters at creating environments of rest and trust that allow Holy Spirit to do surgery on people's minds and hearts. This is what makes us unique and distinct.

Conclusion

John Paul Jackson said, "**Life is all about intimacy with God!** We were created for that. Everything we do should be done with that in mind. If it is not, we will find ourselves burned out, broken, lame, and empty because it is not good for man to be alone. We were created for relationship, specifically with our heavenly Father. Nothing in this world or on the next one is as important as our relationship with God."

Prayer Power

Abba, Father, thank You for creating me for a unique purpose. I confess that for much of my life, the light switch has been turned off and I have been living for myself instead of for You. I acknowledge that "Life is all about intimacy with God!" I acknowledge that "being on-purpose is a lifestyle and means being Christ-like more of the time." I need and want Your help to live my life with passion and purpose for You. Remove whatever barriers are keeping me from doing that. Help me to stay equally yoked to You (Matthew 11:29-30). Bless me to finish the race strong so that at the end I hear You say, "Well done, good and faithful servant" (Matthew 5:21). In Jesus' name I pray. Amen and hallelujah!

Study Guide

Questions:

Q: Why is a two-word purpose statement so valuable?
A: Two-word statements are easy to remember and are thus actionable. They reflect the DNA of our spirit. They keep your purpose simple, making it easy to discern if you are on-purpose or off-purpose.

Q: What is the simple formula for creating an extraordinary life?
A: Live with purpose. Live by priority. Live for productivity.

Q: What are five things to accelerate your big dreams?
A: Mindset, clarity and focus, SMARTT goals, a coach, and a dream team

Q: Which of these five are you lacking and what do you plan to do about that?

_____
_____
_____

Simple Action Step:

Watch Kevin McCarthy's video about "The Power of a Two-Word Purpose Statement." Then write your own personal two-word purpose statement.

www.2wordpurpose.com.

Please be aware that when you come to this web page, it takes about seven minutes before the video starts to play automatically. There is no way to manually advance to the start of the video.

My Story of Finding Time Freedom

A Journey of Adventure

"Do not go where the path may lead. Go instead where there is no path and leave a trail."

—Ralph Waldo Emerson

In his TED video, Simon Sinek says, "All the great and inspiring leaders and organizations in the world think, act, and communicate in the exact same way!" They start with their WHY and then and only then do they work their way out of the Golden Circle to the how and the what.

So I am going to start with my why—why I am so passionate about coaching you to have time freedom.

My Journey of Being Set Free

For the first 20 years of my training and career, I was in a time trap. While I typically only worked 45-50 per week as an anesthesiologist, my hours and work schedule were quite sporadic.

I was called back to the hospital to care for patients many a day and night. There were numerous occasions I did not see the daylight for 12 days in a row because of my work and call schedule.

Many nights I had only a few hours of sleep before having to report back to the operating rooms to begin the cycle again. And there were many weekends when I was called back to the hospital three or four times in a day, each time for hours on end.

Sometimes I was so tired I had to ask one of the operating room nurses to tap me on the shoulder if they noticed I was falling asleep while caring for a patient. And yet I was not allowed to refer a patient to another hospital if I felt I was too tired to be safe. I knew something needed to change.

In the summer of 1998, I read Stephen Covey's book *First Things First*. For me that book was a real eye opener because it talked about fitting in the most important things in your life first, not just more things. I realized I did not even have time to read life-changing books like that.

So I decided I was definitely going to have a change and get out of the rat race. I made a choice to stop trading time for money. Doing that turned out to be more difficult than I anticipated.

After spending a year trying to work out an agreement with my anesthesia colleague to cut back to part-time and failing to do so, I finally gave a seven-week notice and left Culpeper Hospital in July 1999. When I did, **I felt like I had been let out of jail after 20 years**. All of a sudden I was free of the beeper leash and my life was my life again.

It took courage to step away from my bread-and-butter job, from the familiar, into my dream. But once I did, a whole new vista of opportunities opened for me.

Let me summarize my journey to time freedom. First, I recognized I had a problem with my time. That was awareness. Second, I decided I was going to have a change. That was commitment. Third, I wrote my commitment down and put a date to it. In other words, I set a clear, written goal. Fourth, I took action to achieve my goal. Faith without action is dead. And fifth, I overcame fear and stepped out in faith when things did not work out as I had planned.

Benefits of My New Time Freedom

In the Fall of 1999, I joined my parents in Europe for a three week vacation. That was something I had wanted to do for many years because I had grown up in Europe and had not been back for more than 20 years.

While in Italy, we visited with Rosa and her five grown children. Rosa was the live-in nanny for our family when I was a little boy growing up in Italy. She was like a second mom to me. When I returned to Italy, not only did Rosa treat me like one of her kids, but her children all treated me like I was one of their siblings. Wow!

In early 2000, I began reading *The Greatest Salesman in the World* by Og Mandino. Instead of just reading that book one time, each month I read one of the 10 scrolls (chapters) out loud three times per day for 30 days. By the end of the year, after 10 months of doing this, I had most of the book memorized. From this book, I learned the importance of habits and discovered my life purpose. That is priceless.

In the middle of 2000, I met Pastor Mark Jarvis, who was the first person ever in my life to open a Bible and read it to me believing it was true. This was despite the fact that I had gone to church nearly every week for my entire life.

Soon, with Mark's guidance, I began reading the Bible daily on my own for the first time in my life. As a result of that and other extraordinary events and circumstances, I committed my life to Jesus on January 6, 2001. That was the best day of my life. Within a year of that, my wife and two kids experienced their own spiritual rebirths. That too is priceless.

Fruit of Committing My Life to Jesus

After committing my life to Jesus, my world turned right-side up. Things that had never made sense to me, all of a sudden started making sense. My priorities, habits, closest friends, and reason for working changed dramatically.

I went back and practiced anesthesia part-time for six years, but this time for a different reason, to glorify God. As a result, my impact was much greater and I had many extraordinary experiences. Because of my joy and the fruitfulness of my life, one operating room nurse told me, "Dr. Peck, you should write a book titled *Another Day in the Life of Dr. Peck.*"

In late 2001, I joined a Christian accountability group that met in person weekly for five years. Surrounding myself with big thinkers helped me grow enormously.

In January 2002, I began the wonderful habit of daily journaling, which soon became the lead domino of my life. As a result of this habit, I now have written thousands of articles and several books with many more on the way.

In the Fall of 2003, God opened the door for me to work part-time at Giles Memorial Hospital, a hospital in Virginia I did not even know existed beforehand. This was the best anesthesia job of my career.

For the next three years, I worked at a place I loved and was paid like my full-time job before, but only worked two and a half days per week. I had four-day weekends every week and could take one to two week vacations whenever I wanted. Now that was time and financial freedom.

For the first year I worked in Giles County, I stayed two days a week at a gorgeous and luxurious bread and breakfast place overlooking the New River. The view and scenery were breathtaking.

In 2004, I began my own daily TV show called *A Life of Blessing*. That aired two to three times per day, seven days a week in Culpeper, Virginia, the community where I live. The producers of that TV show told me they received more favorable feedback from that TV show than all their other TV shows combined.

In 2007 I stepped away from my best job ever to take a sabbatical year in obedience to Holy Spirit. That was an idea I had never entertained before in my life.

During that sabbatical year, I enrolled in a year-long training program to become a leadership coach. That opened the door for me to start coaching leaders privately and in small groups and to start online coaching programs.

One of the 12-week tracks during my coach training was called *Life Focus*. That helped lay out a path for the rest of my life. Upon reflecting on my life, where I had been and where I was going, I realized my greatest joy came from coaching others to reach their full potential.

During my *Life Focus* training, I was asked to write down a few of my favorite experiences in my life. This helped me realize the Lifeforming Leadership Coach Training was my favorite training ever.

I also realized the weekly coaching group I was a part of for five years from 2001-2005 was a highlight for my life. I remembered Michael Stay, one of my coaching partners, telling me in 2001, "Joseph, you would make a great coach for executives!" Matt Gregory, another coaching partner, told me, "Joseph, your greatest gift is coaching, not the web." This was despite the fact that I had become an internet marketing expert.

I recalled how I met Dr. Jerry Graham on June 1, 2007, the first day of my formal coach training. We soon became good friends and for three years, Jerry was my top coach and mentor. That was wonderful because Jerry is one of the most experienced destiny coaches in the world. Jerry played a key role in keeping me moving forward in my purpose and destiny.

Time freedom allowed me to go places I had never been, meet people I had never met, and do things I had never done.

For example, in 2007 I went with my wife Julia to Lake Tahoe, Nevada to watch her compete in the Xterra National Triathlon Championships. We did that to celebrate our 25th wedding anniversary. The photo of Julia overlooking Lake Tahoe on the front cover of this book is very special to me and came from that extraordinary vacation.

The photo reminds me of our first 25 years of marriage and is a vivid reminder of the importance of slowing down to rest, reflect, and appreciate the beauty and wonder of creation and our Creator.

There is a miracle story behind how I ended up on that mountain to take the photo. To start our vacation, my wife and I flew into Reno, Nevada. When we went to pick up our rental car, we were told all the small cars were gone and that all they could give us was a large minivan. I reluctantly accepted that and we drove to Lake Tahoe.

When Julia and I stopped at the bike shop where her mountain bike had been shipped and reassembled for the race, I suddenly fell in love with mountain biking as we talked with the owner of the store. So I decided to rent a bike and because we had the minivan to carry the bikes, I was able to drive with Julia to a place where we could climb the mountain and access the Xterra race course more easily.

What is so amazing about this story is that God cleared the way for me to go with Julia on that bicycle trail to honor her and have lots of fun in the process. Seven years later, the Lord inspired me to use that photo for the front cover of this book to lead millions of people to slow down to know Him.

In 2009, Julia and I went to Hawaii for two weeks, where she competed in the Xterra World Triathlon Championships. This was a special opportunity to honor my wife and watch her compete in a world championship event with other world-class athletes. Previously, that was something I had only watched on TV, but now I was living that exciting life.

While in Hawaii, we had the opportunity to visit family members on Julia's side of the family, who I had never met. We also were invited to stay in a luxurious condo in downtown Honolulu for free with some good friends of Julia's mother.

I am not writing this to brag about myself, but rather to encourage you to take risks to pursue your God-given dreams.

As Andre Guide once said, "Man cannot discover new oceans unless he has the courage to lose sight of the shore." Let me repeat and personalize this, "You cannot discover new oceans unless you have the courage to lose sight of the shore."

So let me ask you, "How big is your why?"

- Why do you want time freedom?
- What are you going to do with your extra time?
- What do you want to do that you cannot do now?
- What do you want to do that you have never done?
- Who do you want to meet that you have never met?
- Where do you want to go that you have never been?
- What would you do if you had all the time and money to pursue your dreams with passion?
- What is your legacy going to be?

You see, when your why is big enough, the how will work itself out. God is inviting you into an extraordinary opportunity to live a bigger life, but first you must take action and seize the moment.

Prayer Power

Heavenly Father, I praise You as the God of turnarounds. Thank You for guiding Dr. Joseph Peck on his faith journey and leading him to share his encouraging story with me. I know You have something big planned for me too. Bless me to be strong and of good courage (Joshua 1:9) to cross over into my Promised Land. I want to live in a "land flowing with milk and honey" (Leviticus 20:24). I know that requires total surrender. I need and want Your help to do that. In Jesus' name I pray. Amen and hallelujah!

OPPORTUNITY TO
REDEEM YOUR TIME

"Twenty years from now you will be more disappointed by the things that you did not do than by the ones you did do. So throw off the bowlines. Sail away from the safe harbor. Catch the trade winds in your sails. Explore, dream, discover!"

—H. Jackson Brown Jr.

Are you hungry for more and want help from an experienced coach to redeem your precious gift of time? If so, then I invite you to an uncommon opportunity.

Your breakthrough begins with a choice. The reason I shared my story of finding time freedom is to create a desire in you to go on a similar journey. As a dream coach and someone who has successfully navigated my way out of the rat race, I feel confident I can help set you free to live your dreams.

Let me ask you:

- Are you too busy to enjoy your life?
- Is life passing you by too fast?
- Have you had enough of feeling overwhelmed?
- Do you need help eliminating time wasters?
- Are you living below your potential?
- Are you ready to conquer your fears to live a life of fun and adventure?
- Are you willing to do whatever it takes to break through?
- Are you able to invest time, money, and energy to passionately pursue your dreams?

If so, let me introduce you to the...

I Was Busy, Now I am Not Coaching Program

The purpose of this coaching program is to dramatically change the way you think about time to help you redeem your time and accomplish far more than you ever thought possible. When you change your thinking, you change your life.

We help you live a happier, healthier, and more successful life by coaching you to simplify your complicated life, establish healthy habits, prioritize what is most important, and focus.

Since time is your life, you must be a good steward with your time to live your dreams as God intends. How you steward your time determines your impact.

In his book *How to Win Friends and Influence People*, Dale Carnegie said the deepest urge in human nature is the desire to be important. So I know you want to feel important and make a big difference.

Amazingly, you have the exact same number of hours per day as Michelangelo, Thomas Jefferson, Helen Keller, Albert Einstein, Mother Teresa, Bill Gates, and Oprah.

If you let me, I can help you reach for the stars by establishing good habits, having time to reflect, and getting clear on where you are and where you want to go.

Common benefits of the *I Was Busy, Not I am Not*™ coaching program include:

- Redeeming your time by learning to ask simple focusing questions each day.
- Clearly identifying time wasters and eliminating them. We help you become aware of how you are allocating your time, so you invest your time wisely rather than spending it foolishly.
- Experiencing the power of less, allowing you to accomplish more by doing less and focusing on the most important things.
- Establishing new habits to increase your productivity and effectiveness.
- Developing a one year growth calendar to accomplish more in a year. Our approach helps you learn faster from your mistakes and become a better planner.
- Setting SMARTT Goals for your year, months, weeks, and days to live on purpose
- Enjoying a closer walk with God
- And so much more!

We know the *I Was Busy, Not I am Not*™ coaching program is effective. Here are things participants have said:

> "This coaching program was a key piece for me with what God has called me to do. I am seeing new ideas and new ways of looking at my business unfold before me."
>
> **—Marlee Huber**

> "The whole idea of focus is crucial! I am refining, re-evaluating, and reformatting my tasks, responsibilities, and goals."
>
> **—Glenn Hart**

> "For me it was a big wake up call to help me be conscious about what I was doing with my time and what signals I was sending about how I was using my time. I realized there had been a gap between what I was saying was important and what my behaviors were actually demonstrating with the truth of what was important."
>
> **—Tara Connell**

> "I have changed my thinking about time. That has helped me eliminate time wasters and put the big rocks in the jar of my life first. I am now asking questions like 'What is the most important thing?' and 'Where should we be focusing our time?'"
>
> **—Steve Connell**

> "The whole course was about stewarding time in such a way we can live on purpose!"
>
> **—Tara Martin**

There are at least two things that make this coaching program unique:

1. We integrate time coaching and dream coaching, teaching you to be a good steward with your time, while also empowering your dreams.
2. We teach you how to journal to hear God's voice more clearly for both your personal and work life. This brings clarity and focus to live an extraordinary life.

PERSONAL INVITATION

If you are too busy and want more time to live your big dreams, I would like to personally invite you to participate in my life-changing *I Was Busy, Now I'm Not*™ coaching program to discover how to simplify your complicated life, make time for what matters most, and live your big dreams.

To learn more, please visit www.moretime777.com

Prayer Power

Heavenly Father, thank You for this opportunity to learn and to grow. Thank You for Your inspiration and revelation. LORD, I know You are at work all around me. Help me to tune into Your frequency to join You in what You are already doing. Help me to stop making excuses for why I do not have enough time. Help me to make a commitment to find time for what matters most. Create a sense of urgency in me to redeem my time.

Father God, I want to be part of a dream team with a culture full of courage to face the impossible, love that overcomes fear, and the tangible presence and power of God that makes the supernatural a daily experience. Bless me with an environment in which people genuinely know and commit to help one another discover the gold You put in each of us and then to walk alongside each other to see the fullness of that gold expressed. In Jesus' name, we pray and give You thanks. Amen and hallelujah!

Blessings to redeem your time and pursue your big dreams!

Recommended Resources

"Life should be lived passionately. Otherwise you're playing another person's game."

—Lewis Howes

Online Resources

This book is static (i.e., once the book is printed, no more changes can be made to it easily). However, we have a wealth of growing online resources, including audios, videos, webinars, etc., to help you redeem your time and live your big dreams.

To join our community and stay connected, we encourage you to subscribe to the *I Was Busy, Now I'm Not* blog and follow us on Facebook, LinkedIn, Twitter, and other social media platforms. Here are the links to do so:

- www.iwasbusynowimnot.com
- www.facebook.com/iwbnin
- www.twitter.com/iwbnin
- www.linkedin.com/groups?gid=8113867

Books

1) *The On-Purpose Person: Making Your Life Make Sense* by Kevin W. McCarthy

The number one time waster by far is not living on purpose. This is the best book I have ever read to help people discover and simplify their life purpose.

Is your life filled, yet unfulfilled? Do you feel pulled in a thousand different directions? Are your days so busy you hardly have time to think? Are you living up to other people's expectations while your own plans and dreams go unmet? In *The On-Purpose Person* you will learn how to discover who you are, where you are headed, what you should do, and what is most important to you! That is being on-purpose! Tap into your highest potential with *The On-Purpose Person*.

2) *The ONE Thing: The Surprisingly Simple Truth behind Extraordinary Results* by Gary Keller

The key to redeeming your time is focus. This is the best book I have ever read to develop focus. Gary defines leadership as "teaching people how to think the way they need to think so they can do what they need to do when they need to do it, so they can get what they want when they want it."

YOU WANT LESS. You want fewer distractions and less on your plate. The daily barrage of e-mails, texts, tweets, messages, and meetings distract you and stress you out. The simultaneous demands of work and family are taking a toll. And what's the cost? Second-rate work, missed deadlines, smaller paychecks, fewer promotions—and lots of stress.

AND YOU WANT MORE. You want more productivity from your work—more income for a better lifestyle. You want more satisfaction from life, and more time for yourself, your family, and your friends.

Now you can have both—less and more.

In *The ONE Thing*, you will learn to:

- cut through the clutter
- achieve better results in less time
- build momentum toward your goal
- dial down the stress
- overcome that overwhelmed feeling
- revive your energy
- stay on track
- master what matters to you

The ONE Thing delivers extraordinary results in every area of your life—work, personal, family, and spiritual. What is your one thing?

3) *Conquer Fear* by Lisa Jimenez

Lisa Jimenez says "Fear is the dominant problem in your life today." This is the best book about conquering fear and overcoming procrastination I have read.

Learn how you can break through fear by developing a Biblically-based, powerful belief system. You really can live a richer, more faith-filled life.

4) *4 Keys to Hearing God's Voice* by Mark Virkler

Dr. Mark Virkler, founder of Communion with God Ministries and Christian Leadership University, has written more than 50 books and taught hundreds of thousands of people how to hear God's voice. This is his best-selling book ever and for good reason. People are hungry to hear God.

This book is both practical and inspirational, combining the best of the school of the Word and the school of the Spirit to hear God's voice.

5) *Secrets of the Vine: Breaking Through to Abundance* by Dr. Bruce Wilkinson

In this powerful follow-up to his bestseller *The Prayer of Jabez*, Dr. Bruce Wilkinson explores John 15 to show readers how to make maximum impact for God. Dr. Wilkinson demonstrates how Jesus is the Vine of life, discusses four levels of "fruit bearing" (doing the good work of God), and reveals three life-changing truths that will lead readers to new joy and effectiveness in His kingdom. *Secrets of the Vine* opens readers' eyes to the Lord's hand in their lives and uncovers surprising insights that will point them toward a new path of consequence for God's glory.

6) *You 2 (Squared): A High Velocity Formula for Multiplying Your Personal Effectiveness in Quantum Leaps* by Price Pritchett

This book promotes an unconventional, quantum leap strategy for achieving breakthrough performance. This powerful new method replaces the concept of attaining gradual, incremental success through massive effort. Instead, it puts forth 18 key components for building massive success while expending less effort.

7) *How To Hear God: Keys To Hearing God's Voice Every Day (Christian Life Coaching Guide)* by Lynne Lee

The big secret about hearing God's voice is...there is no secret! The fact is, God wants you to hear Him even more than you want to hear Him. He even promises that His sheep (that's us!) will hear His voice. Anybody can hear from God. In fact, you hear God every day; you just don't always recognize that it is God speaking to you. This practical, inspiring coaching guide equips you to recognize God's voice, even if your prayer life is currently weak or non-existent.

8) *The Greatest Salesman in the World* by Og Mandino

Next to the Bible, this best-selling book had a greater impact on me than any other book I have ever read.

What you are today is not important, for in this runaway bestseller you will learn how to change your life by applying the secrets in 10 ancient scrolls.

9) *If How-To's Were Enough We Would All Be Skinny, Rich, and Happy* by Brian Klemmer

In this results-getting book, Brian Klemmer explores what is missing and the real reason why most people do not succeed. The secret is found in seven paradigms that will change the course of your life.

10) *The Precious Present* by Spencer Johnson, M.D.

Most people are not content living in the moment, but that is the secret to happiness. A simple story, engagingly told, *The Precious Present* does more than capture the heart; it is a valuable gift for anyone seeking a deeper level of fulfillment and personal happiness.

11) *The Millionaire Messenger: Make a Difference and a Fortune Sharing Your Advice* by Brendon Burchard

You can light the way for others. In this game-changing book by Brendon Burchard, founder of Experts Academy, you will discover:

- Your life story and experience have greater importance and market value than you probably ever dreamed.
- You are here to make a difference in this world. The best way to do that is to package your knowledge and advice (on any topic, in any industry) to help others succeed.
- You can get paid for sharing your advice and how-to information, and in the process you can build a lucrative business and a profoundly meaningful life.

12) *Practicing His Presence (The Library of Spiritual Classics, Volume 1)* by Brother Lawrence and Frank Laubach

If you wish to know your LORD in a deeper way, you are invited to join the vast host of Christians who, over three centuries, have turned to this book more than any other—except the Scriptures—in order to begin that journey to the depths of Christ.

Life-Changing Webinars (Videos)

All of these can be found at www.empower2000.com/store

1) *Redeeming the Time* with Rick Grubbs
   Simple Solutions for Success in Life
2) *Sacred Time—Sacred Place* with Patricia King
   Co-laboring and Co-creating With God
3) *Applying The Power Of Less* with Steve and Tara Connell
   Priorities and Habits to Put First Things First
4) *Developing Your One Year Growth Calendar*
   Planning to Succeed
5) *Setting SMARTT Goals*
   Turning Goals Into Action Items
6) *Uncommon Journaling For Divine Destiny*
   Experiencing God in Extraordinary Ways For Extraordinary Fruit
7) *Conquer Fear*
   Stop Defeating Yourself—End Self-Sabotage
8) *The 60-60 Experiment*
   Staying Connected to God

Acknowledgments

Rejoice always; pray without ceasing; In everything give thanks; for this is the will of God in Christ Jesus for you. (1 Thessalonians 5:16-18)

Like icing on a cake, I have saved the best for last. There are many people who have had a positive impact on me and how I steward my time, but none more so than my parents, my wife, my children, Pastor Mark Jarvis, Pastor Matt Gregory, and Michael Stay.

People are listed in chronological order here according to when they became a part of my life.

Thank you Darrell and Jane Peck for sharing the love of God with me throughout my lifetime and for always making family a priority. Thank you for modeling a non-busy, productive lifestyle and for teaching me the value of planning.

Thank you Julia for our 33 years of marriage and for all your support, encouragement, and accountability to help me grow and become the leader I am today. Thank you for your patience in my journey to discover and function from my "sweet spot."

Thank you Caren and Robbie for making our family a priority and for the many important lessons you have taught me over your lifetimes.

Thank you Pastor Mark Jarvis for leading me to a personal relationship with Jesus, teaching me what it means to be a champion for Christ, and helping me understand that the best way to multiply my time is to give more time to God.

Thank you Matt Gregory for being a part of my first coaching group for five years, serving as my pastor for eight years, helping me grow in many healthy ways, for blessing my family, and for telling me my greatest gift is coaching.

Thank you Michael Stay for being a part of my first coaching group, for modeling servant leadership, for taking me through several strategic planning processes, and for telling me I would make a great coach for executives.

Thank you Mark Jenkins for your leadership as pastor of Mountain View Community Church. So many of your messages have been on target and on time to lead me in the way everlasting (Psalm 139:23-24). I appreciate your love for God, for your family, and for people, as well as your boldness to preach the truth in love.

Thank you Virginia Morton for being a loyal friend, powerful prayer partner, and leader in our community. I look forward to seeing *Marching Through Culpeper* on the big screen in the future.

Thank you Chaplain Liz Danielsen for modeling a life of Christian service while maintaining a healthy work-life balance. I believe Spiritual Care Support Ministries will become the pre-eminent provider of services and products for the ill, dying, and bereaved.

Thank you Jack Stagman for being one of the best friends and encouragers a man could ever hope for. You are one of the most generous people I have ever known and have radically changed my life. I believe God is positioning you as one of the preeminent leaders in the world to transform governments and nations.

Thank you Dr. Joseph Umidi for the many ways you have encouraged and inspired me. The Lifeforming Leadership Coaching was the best training of my entire life.

Thank you Dr. Jerry Graham for serving as my top coach and mentor for three years and for encouraging me to continue to pursue my dreams despite the many challenges.

Thank you Dr. Mark Virkler for teaching me the four keys to hearing God's voice. Thank you for your friendship, for your valuable teaching resources, and for your priceless coaching and mentoring. Thank you for the extraordinary impact on me and millions of other people around the world.

Thank you Bob Sims for your gifts of time, wisdom, prayers, encouragement, and the financial seed you sowed into my life to help me continue my journey pursuing my dreams.

Thank you Judi Reid for investing in my life and my dreams at such at a high level. Your time, wisdom, expert help, and encouragement have been priceless to me. Your counsel to focus on using my gift of hosting and facilitating webinars has led to so much fruit, including publishing this book. Thank you for your help proofreading and editing this book, especially early on, which helped pave the way for this book to be accepted by Morgan James Publishing. I believe *Women of Value* will become a global movement empowering millions of women and their dreams because you model extraordinary value.

Thank you Celene Grace Zulla for providing many of the background services for me during the past three years, allowing me to progress at a much faster rate. Thank you for your patience, prayers, and frequent encouragement.

Thank you Lynne Lee for coaching, encouraging, inspiring, and empowering me to become who I am in Christ to be able to fulfill my destiny. The day I met you was a major turning point in my life. I look forward to seeing how God uses your *How to Hear God* book and coaching program to draw millions of people into closer relationship with Him.

Thank you Renato Amato for your friendship, encouragement, counsel, time, and prayers. You and your ministry have been a big inspiration to me. I will never forget the extraordinary way we met.

Thank you Bertha Hinson for investing in my life at a high level and for serving as a spiritual mother during a critical growth period in my life. I hope to be as energetic and enthusiastic as you when I am your age.

Thank you Nancy Slocum for being a wonderful friend, encourager, counselor, and intercessor. Your prayers are always so anointed and the prophetic words you shared before several live webinars prepared the way for much good fruit.

Thank you Janet Daughtry for your outstanding Breakthrough Life Coach training. Within months of enrolling in that, so many major breakthroughs happened in my life, including restarting my coaching for my son and creating my *30 Days to Breakthrough* e-coaching program. Thank you for the webinars we did together, especially the one about "Renewing the Mind." You are an extraordinary coach, teacher, and servant leader.

Thank you Dr. Bruce Cook for the many ways you have blessed me and for opening so many doors of opportunity. I am forever grateful for the time and wisdom you sowed into my life.

Thank you Michael Oswald for your faithful friendship, servant leadership, and expertise as General Counsel for Empower 2000. Thank you for helping prepare the study guide for this book and for your assistance in proofreading the book. You have been like a "Joseph" to me, a channel of God's wisdom. You epitomize what a great attorney can be.

Thank you Larry Tyler for encouraging, coaching, and challenging me to succeed so greatly that only God could get the credit. Your endorsement of me as "the maestro making the entire orchestra play with one voice" is my favorite ever. Thank you for your financial generosity in my times of need.

Thank you Dr. Gordon Bradshaw for your inspiration, revelations, frequent encouragement, and edifying books. You have always made me feel like I belonged. Thank you for modeling outstanding apostolic leadership.

Thank you Marnie Pehrson for setting such a great example of integrity in the internet marketing world. Thank you for all you taught me, for building my confidence, and for the many doors you opened for me. Thank you for asking the life-changing question, "If you knew you were going to die tomorrow and somebody gave you a megaphone to deliver one message today, what would it be?" My answer to that now is "Time is your life!" Thank you being a light-bearer for me and so many others.

Thank you Steve Connell for serving as my top business coach over the past three years and for helping me get clear on my vision, mission, and values. You and Tara are truly master communicators and relationship experts.

Thank you Russel Stauffer for serving as a reformer bringing creative people, ideas, and finances together for extraordinary change no one ever thought possible. You truly are a master joint venture broker. Of all the people I have ever met, you are one of the biggest dreamers and the best role model for speaking "words of life."

Thank you Ken McArthur for your humble servant leadership in the internet marketing, joint venture space and for the gift of your time and friendship. I am forever grateful for your jvAlert Live event in Crystal City, Virginia, and my new friendships that resulted, including the one with David Hancock, my publisher.

Thank you Sharon Billins for your powerful prophetic words, love, encouragement, and prayers. Your ability to see someone's life and speak out their destiny the first time you meet them is profound. Thank you for serving as a spiritual mother for me.

Thank you Jackie Seeno for your enthusiasm, inspiration, and encouragement. The journal you gave me as a gift in Atlanta and the note you wrote in the front of that have turned out to be priceless. That was the best gift you could have ever given me.

Thank you Dr. John Burpee for your time and friendship and for serving as one of my top coaches and mentors during the past few years. Thank you for Empowering Expectation and Bridging Destiny for me.

Thank you Gary Beaton for your words of life and prophetic insights, inspiration, revelation, and illumination. Thank you for serving as one of my top apostolic prophetic intercessors.

Thank you Robert and Cheryl-Ann Needham for coaching me, for connecting me with Kevin McCarthy, and for "stewarding the stewards." Thank you Cheryl-Ann for *Sound Alignment*, which is one of the most profound books on unity I have ever read.

Thank you Kevin W. McCarthy for *The On-Purpose Person* book and for your private coaching to help me get clear on my two-word purpose statements. That made a profound difference in my life and focus.

Thank you Dr. Tony Dale for your friendship, humility, generosity, and servant leadership. You epitomize what a physician can be and can do when he is centered in Christ. I believe The Health Coop is God's answer to the "Affordable Care Act."

Thank you David Sluka for your assistance designing the book cover, for your priceless counsel to ensure this book is professional, and for your proofreading. It is easy to understand why you have been successful at hitthemarkpublishing.com.

Thank you Scott Shofner for the gift of your friendship and mentoring to build my faith and trust in God. Thank you for the regular reminder in your email signature that "God is good and life is a gift."

Thank you Vic Johnson for your coaching and mentoring in *The Champions Club*. That has been one of the best business investments I ever made. You have helped me overcome many limiting beliefs I was not aware of before. Thank you for the 12-week Maximum Momentum course in the last quarter of 2013 which created the momentum to write and publish this book and re-launch my *I Was Busy, Now I am Not*™ coaching program.

Thank you David Hancock for believing in me, this book, and my dream to help millions of people around the world become better stewards with their time and live their dreams. Thank you for opening the gate for this book to be published and marketed by Morgan James Publishing. It is easy for me to see why you are "recognized by NASDAQ as one of the world's most prestigious business leaders and reported to be the future of publishing."

Thank you Rick and Joey Saunders for your love, kindness, inspiration, revelation, and coaching. You have one of the most beautiful marriages I have seen and your ability to hear God's voice clearly is extraordinary. I believe God is positioning Lord and Saunders Real Estate to be one of the preeminent real estate companies in the world.

Thank you to the many people who have participated in my coaching programs and Master's Mind Marketing™ tribes. I have learned more from you than you have from me.

And finally, thank you to my extended family, friends, and thousands of followers. Your support and encouragement have meant so much to me.

A SPECIAL TRIBUTE
TO MY FATHER

Over the years, I have come to discover that many people did not have a loving father. Some fathers are absent, abusive, addictive, apathetic, authoritarian, passive, or unavailable.

But my father was always there for me. I do not remember a single day in my life where I did not feel loved by him. Consequently, it has always been easy for me to believe in a loving God.

When I was growing up, my father took our family to church nearly every weekend. He did not quote scriptures often, but he modeled the book of Proverbs to me and our family. When I began reading the Bible regularly in my forties, many of the Proverbs reminded me of my father. For example, every time I read *Proverbs 13:22—A good man leaves an inheritance to his children's children—*I think of my father.

My father always made family a high priority. Despite his positions of leadership in the U.S. Army and at the Pentagon, he was home for dinner on time nearly every day. He always said a prayer before meal time.

When I was an adult, my father planned regular family gatherings for our whole family. Whenever, we went to visit my parents, we could count on good family meals and good conversation. My father and mother came to nearly every special occasion for my immediate family.

My father is an extremely humble man. He never bragged about any of his accomplishments, either personal or at work. When I stepped away from my full-time job as an anesthesiologist in 1999 and started Empower 2000, I asked my father if he would serve as Secretary for my company. When he agreed, I asked if he had a resume. He told me "no," but said he did have a Washington Post article from 1994 summarizing the second half of his career.

When I saw that, I was blown away. I was completely unaware of my father's tremendous accomplishments. For example, that newspaper article stated: "Unquestionably, the single area for which Mr. Peck is most widely renowned is Government ethics. He was the Army's Designated Agency Ethics Official and served as overall manager of the Army's ethics program for over 15 years, planning and directing the program since the Ethics in Government Act of 1978 first took effect. Under his direction, the Army's program has been widely recognized as among the best, Government-wide. Many of its features have been adopted by the Department of Defense and other departments. Demonstrating his recognized preeminence in this area, he is the only person invited to chair a panel at every national Government Ethics conference, from the first in 1980 through its latest in 1993."

I say this not to brag, but to show the value of humility and the environment I grew up in. *By humility and the fear of the LORD are riches and honor and life. (Proverbs 22:4)*

My father is a good listener. It took me more than 40 years to understand and appreciate the value of that.

My father never pressured me to do anything or to pursue any specific career. He simply asked good questions to help me make better choices. He was there for me whenever I needed him.

When I went through financial challenges during my transition from working as a physician to a leadership coach, my father was there to help me out. Even though some of my decisions frustrated him, he never gave up on me or turned his back on me.

My father modeled a godly marriage. When I was going through a difficult season in my marriage, my father told me when two people get married, they become "one flesh" (Ephesians 5:31). That helped me realize when I said negative things to my wife or about her that I was actually hurting myself as well as both of us.

My father taught me by example that the best father is a good husband and the best husband is a good father.

As Abraham Lincoln said, "A good example is worth a thousand sermons." Thank you Dad for being a great father and role model. And thank you Mom for being a great mother and Dad's best friend. You helped him be a great success.

Prayer Power

Father God, thank You for the precious gift of a loving father and mother. May this tribute to my earthly father inspire many other fathers and mothers to be the best parents they can be for their children. May you use this tribute to "turn the hearts of the fathers to the children, and the hearts of the children to their fathers" (Malachi 4:6). In Jesus' name, I pray. Amen and hallelujah!

THE SOUND OF
THE TRUMPET: 222

On a Sunday in early January 2011, three unusual things happened in a single day to make "222" jump out at me.

First, when I went to the 7-Eleven in Culpeper to get gas, I noticed a banner across the front of the store entrance that read "$2.22" for three things. I asked the Lord, "Why did you have me notice that?"

Later that afternoon when I was driving back home after an open house for a new child center addition at a big church, I looked down at my car clock. It said "2:22." That was the first and only time I looked at my car clock that day.

Later that evening, I called one of my clients to make plans to meet the next day. He told me he was not available because he had to go to the hospital to visit his administrative assistant who was on her death bed. When I asked what room she was in at the hospital, he told me "2222."

A few days later, my friend Renato Amato in Italy posted a new article on his blog titled "WFJ: Your sound of the trumpet: 222!" Renato knew nothing about what had transpired with me a few days earlier. Here is what Renato wrote:

> In the recent weeks I have heard the voice of the Lord more than once, speaking to my heart and saying: "222!!! That's the sound of the trumpet for your life: 2 Timothy 2:2!"

> "The things that you have heard of Me, teach them to faithful men who shall be able to teach them to others also!"

> Those who know us well also know that our passion has always been to pour God's healing balm of love on those whose hearts are broken because of life's stormy events. This desire that God placed in our hearts since we were young has always been the steady helm of our journey in this world, no matter the events or changes around us …

In a recent WFJ message titled "New Year 2011: Be led by the Spirit!", the Lord told us that "**The thoughts and intents of your heart (Heb. 4:12) are like a rudder directing your life.** As long as it's pointed in the right direction, the waves of the sea and surrounding winds will only push you in the same direction and you will reach your destination. The important thing is to stand firm in your values and beliefs, so that I can help you land on the right bank."

Beside the encouragement that we usually receive through the "Words From Jesus (WJF)" that He whispers to our hearts, the Lord knew that we also needed the "sound of a trumpet" loud and clear that would show us the direction to follow in this New Year 2011! Here it is:

(**WFJ** = Words from Jesus): 222! That's the sound of the trumpet for your life: **"Teach Others TO Teach Others" (2 Timothy 2:2)!** T.O. TO T.O. You were created for this, not only to teach others "the things you have heard from Me" in the past, but also those that you continue to hear from Me, when "*it's not you that speak, but the Spirit of My Father speaking through you" (Matthew 10:20)*!

I want you to Teach Others TO Teach Others to be led by Me, allowing My Spirit to work in and through them. I want you TO Teach Others TO hear My voice, to follow the whispers of My Spirit and learn to be led by Me in everything! Being *"led by My Spirit" (Rom. 8:14)* is what many of My children need to learn, and you can "Teach Others TO Teach Others" to be led by My Spirit in everything they do, so they don't try to manage other people's lives by telling them what to do, but allow My Spirit to lead My sheep along *"the green pastures and fresh waters" (Psalm 23:2)* that will quench their thirst!

Teach Others TO Teach Others to be led by My Spirit! A church led by the Spirit is what the world needs! People need leaders who are led by Me, *"the Author and Finisher of their faith" (Heb. 12:2)*, not by their own thoughts and minds! When a leader uses his knowledge to be praised by men, he's not being "led by My Spirit," because I'm not in that motivation! When a leader uses his knowledge to manipulate people's lives, instead of encouraging them to look to Me, he is not being "led by My Spirit," because I do not operate that way.

A humble servant who is yielded to My Spirit and led by My love for the lost, by My desire to touch lives with My love and My divine wisdom to Teach Others TO Teach Others, is what I need! That will make you the effective tool that I need, a *"faithful and wise servant, who gives meat to My household" (Matt. 24:45)*, recognizing that it's "My" household, not his! Those who will come to your side to help you build the dream that I have put in your heart, will do it because they are of My household, being led by My Spirit.

"Hold fast that crown" (Rev. 3:11) and continue to Teach Others TO Teach Others, for that knowledge was given for you to share, to Teach Others TO Teach Others! A *"faithful and wise servant, who gives meat to My household in due season" (Matt. 24:45)*, is what you are called to be, using every opportunity to Teach Others TO Teach Others!

If you *"strengthen your brethren" (Luke 22:32)*, you will be strengthening My kingdom! If you Teach Others TO Teach Others, you will bear fruit that will expand and multiply way beyond your life on earth in extraordinary ways!

The law of multiplication is: do not hold back for yourself what you have been given to share with others! *"Cast your bread upon the waters: for one day you shall find it" (Eccl. 11:1)*, and it will delight your heart and give you a taste of how far your life can go if shared with others!

Have faith, I will build your house and will give you the needed tools to fulfill the dreams and purpose that I placed in your heart, the ultimate plan for which you were created!

While journaling in my sacred place during my sacred time, I was inspired to include this important message at the end of my book. Meditate on this and ask the Lord how this applies to your life.

ABOUT THE AUTHOR

Joseph Peck, M.D., is the great connector EMPOWERING DREAMS of millions of people through coaching, journaling, and life-changing webinars.

In addition to being a physician and creative marketing and communication strategist, Dr. Peck is a 30-60-100 Dream Coach, coaching leaders to leverage their time to magnify their impact 30-60-100 fold in 12 months. This gift attracts leaders of integrity and wealth who want to change the world for good and for God.

Dr. Peck is recognized by many as a global thought leader for life-changing webinars to empower dreams, transform communities, and disciple nations. He is passionate about helping people share their stories, ideas, and gifts with the world via webinars because stories are life-changing and webinars are the #1 online marketing, teaching, and connecting tool, bar none. He says webinars are the new global interactive TV.

Dr. Peck is a master at assembling and facilitating high performance dream teams (mastermind groups). He communicates weekly with groups of business and thought leaders around the world.

According to Larry Tyler, a business coach, "Joseph is the maestro, making the entire orchestra speak with one voice! God has called him and given him the gifts and talent to take so many different individuals (instruments & sounds) and blend them together, so disciplined and so coordinated into Sound Alignment."

Dr. Peck is the founder of the Master's Dream Academy. His goal is for that to be the world's premier training center and community to Empower Dreams.

Dr. Peck is a prolific writer, having authored and co-authored several books with many more on the way. He is a popular speaker. Some of his favorite topics to speak about include "Living Big / Mastering Your Life," "I Was Busy, Now I'm Not," "Uncommon Journaling for Divine Destiny," "Master's Mind Marketing," and "Leveraging Your Life and Business with Webinars."

Simple ways to connect with Dr. Peck include:

Websites

www.iwasbusynowimnot.com
www.empower2000.com
www.josephpeck.com

LinkedIn: www.linkedin.com/in/thejournalguy
Facebook: www.facebook.com/thejournalguy
Twitter: www.twitter.com/thejournalguy

Search me, O God, and know my heart; Try me, and know my anxieties; And see if there is any wicked way in me, And lead me in the way everlasting. (Psalm 139:23-24)